WHY DON'T I FEEL OK?

By
Marjorie Umphrey &
Richard Laird

WHY DON'T I FEEL OK?

Copyright © 1977 Harvest House Publishers
Irvine, California 92714
Library of Congress Catalog Card
   Number: 77-024826
ISBN 0-89081-041-9

Printed in the United States of America

This Book is dedicated . . .
         to Cindy and Kirk
      Two very ''okay'' people. Your vitality for
      living and spirit of love demonstrate the
      words of this book.

Acknowledgements
to Dr. Tom Wilson and Diane Momb for their
insipration and instruction in the area of Transactional
Analysis during the past two years.

TABLE OF CONTENTS

Preface

The overall purpose of this book is three-fold:

1. To encourage you to live a satisfying life.
2. To suggest—a method of understanding behavior—Transactional Analysis—the use of which can help you maximize yourself and your relationships.
3. To use the principles of Scripture as a frame of reference.

This is not a book on Transactional Analysis; nor is it a book of theology. Rather, we have attempted to combine the dynamic concepts from both in an attempt to build a long overdue bridge.

The idea evolved out of a need that we have experienced over a period of more than twenty years in the Christian community as well as in the counseling field.

The inspiration came out of our own success story. What we say in these pages has worked for us and for the many others whom we have counseled. The significant, positive results from Transactional

Analysis theory combine with the spiritual benefits of the Christian message brought forth two happy, autonomous Christians. We wish to share these results with you.

The information given on Transactional Analysis is, of necessity, limited. We encourage you to do further study using the list of related literature at the back of the book.

Except for obvious personal illustrations involving our names and the "Cassandra McMillan story," all other names are ficticious. All case studies are prototypes of real life situations, which we regularly encounter in our counseling practice.

We have chosen to alternate between the male-female gender. Because of the dual authorship both "we" and "I" are used interchangeably so as not to interrupt the flow of thought.

Hopefully, barriers are replaced by bridges. We have shared from our private needs and experiences. Our obvious willingness to disclose ourselves will perhaps express to you the element of urgency and caring behind our words.

Marjorie Umphrey, Ph.D.
Richard Laird, Ph.D.
Glendale, California

1

REACH OUT FOR YOU

REACH OUT FOR YOU

The telephone rings in the early hours of the morning and the voice on the other end apologetically says, "I know I shouldn't be saying this, but I can't seem to cope any longer." The soft whimpering voice spends more time apologizing than asking for help or stating the problem. Almost immediately I attempt to interrupt. "Please don't say you're sorry for asking for help," I respond in tones that probably reflect some desperation. "But, I'm a Christian! Don't you see, I'm a Christian." He is almost shouting at me by this time. His voice is still shaky, but as though anger pushes out the tones, he desperately screams. "Christians aren't supposed to have problems—they are supposed to be able to cope!"

By this time, I am a mixture of feelings. I'm annoyed that I have been awakened from a delightful sleep only to hear a theological discussion about what a Christian should or shouldn't do. I'm feeling pain for another human being who is hurting and needing help. I'm feeling helpless because the party on the other end is asking for help and putting up barriers at the same time. I feel confused about how a person in the Christian community can feel such need for perfection.

This is not an isolated case. In fact, this is almost an everyday occurrence. I have stacks of letters in my files from men and women of all faiths who hesitatingly reach out to me for help. Only total desperation moved their hand to write a letter or dial the phone. Only a severe crisis motivated them to say, "Help Me!"

The hesitation of the people in these cases does not seem to stem from any sense of shame. You know what I mean by shame, don't you? It wasn't all that long ago when those who dared to visit a counselor or psychologist would only dare to whisper about it to their closest friend. Even to confide in your minister was a risky move and somewhat unacceptable.

Rather than shame, it seems that many people from a religious community or a strong ethnic community experience the act of reaching out for help as a sign of weakness. This would include: Weakness in oneself, weakness in faith, weakness in one's family, culture or religion, and even weakness in God. Somehow, these people equate asking for help with weakness. When this weakness involves self, family, culture, religion, or God, the emotion of fear complicates the original problem.

Let me explain how I experience this. All of these

things that have been mentioned—such as family, religion, culture, God—are often referred to by psychologists and sociologists as one's support system. This support system has been visualized by some as the pillars holding up the superstructure of one's personality. When any one of these pillars seem shaky or crumbles, it affects us.

When that voice on the telephone screams to me, "But I'm a Christian!" or "But I'm a Catholic!" or "But I had good Jewish parents," I feel that this person has had to deny his support system in order to reach out for help. That support system is important but so is the privilege of reaching out.

Then too, I'm curious about this concept of perfection. How has this been perpetuated? How have we really gone about convincing ourselves and one another that we need to be perfect—or at least we are to pretend to be perfect?

Oh, I don't mean we are perfect in word or deed. I don't run into many people like that. By the time someone comes to me, they are willing to admit they're not perfect.

I'm speaking of being perfect in the sense of needing, feeling, hurting, loving. Don't laugh, we hear this every day: I'm from this background, therefore, I shouldn't need or I shouldn't feel anger or . . . it's wrong for me to hurt like this or to ask for love.

We feel that you do not have to experience these painful feelings of rejection from others or even from yourself. By the same token, you do not need to abandon all that has been real or precious to you, and all that has worked for you. What we will ask you to do in this book is to openly, honestly and with personal candor examine what you really need.

It has been our experience after years of leading seminars and counseling, that people feel very alone. Wait a minute, we are not saying you are by yourself. We are saying that perhaps your real self is lonely. Oh yes, we can anticipate what your response might be. "I should never be alone—God is always with me." Yes, you are right. God is always with you. But can you honestly say you are always able to feel the presence of God with you? Let us be perfectly frank, we quite often find that Christians appear to be the loneliest people we've encountered. Why should this be? Perhaps one of the reasons might be that we are trying to live up to a script that has been handed to us through succeeding well-intended generations.

Let us share with you an example of what we mean by loneliness. In a group that the authors once conducted, one participant was an extremely intellectual, successful and by every definition an "okay person." However, he expressed feelings of separation from others, was constantly defensive and hid his true feelings in many ways. During an encounter with a woman in the group who did not seem to have all his abilities and gifts, she said to him, "The trouble is—you are lonely but you do not know it!" Many of your problems, both minor and major, may be due to loneliness. If you are truly honest, you recognize that you can be alienated from God, others and even yourself and be unaware of it.

Again, let us presuppose what your answer would be to your last statement. "It is sin that separates us from God." We do not feel that this is an adequate explanation for such a universal human dilemma. One of the most common statements we hear is, "My problem is that I'm a sinner." On the other hand, an equally common statement is, "I feel that I'm doing all that God would have me do; yet I still feel lonely."

What is this experience that we call loneliness?

1. Loneliness is a conscious feeling of separation from others.
2. Loneliness is a feeling masked by another feeling such as anger or hate.
3. Loneliness is a driving force toward success that ends in non-fulfillment.
4. Loneliness is repeating behavior over and over with no apparent reason or goal.
5. Loneliness is boredom.
6. Loneliness is an inability to meet your needs.
7. Loneliness is feeling self-conscious.
8. Loneliness is a feeling of rejection.
9. Loneliness is no matter how hard I try I won't be able to succeed.
10. Loneliness is a feeling "I have everything I need."

You can see that loneliness is disguised in many different forms. When you read the list, did at least three or more of those apply to you? If so, then you are experiencing some degree of loneliness.

This is not a book about loneliness. We are simply sharing with you one of the most common problems we encounter. It seems to be the underlying cause of many other problems.

As I write this, I reflect on a particular situation in my own life. One night while conducting a group of which the purpose was to learn to communicate, I suddenly realized the irony of what we were doing. The group consisted of nine people, all of whom had seemingly minor problems. Everyone was talking and there was a lot of laughter. It appeared, however, that no one was really reaching out to touch another person. Inwardly, I reflected on what a tragedy this really was. Nine living, caring, needing human beings struggling so hard to span the distance from one person to another.

What kept them apart? Why couldn't they simply say: I need you! I want to tell you about me! I want to hear about you! But they couldn't. It seemed like they were encased in a tough box of silence. Yes, they could say what was expected of them. They could use the proper words. But they could not unveil the private inner realities of the world in which they lived every day. People are *afraid* to give themselves permission to be who they are.

Stop for a moment and ask yourself some questions:

1. Do you have a person to whom you can disclose yourself?

2. Do you experience yourself as honest in your social relations?
3. Do you pattern yourself after another person or persons?
4. Are you really living your own life or is someone living it for you?
5. Are you playing a role?
6. Do you feel a need to reflect a certain image?
7. Are you fearful of encountering yourself?
8. Are you living your life the way you want to live it?
9. Are you afraid of taking the responsibilities for your own decisions?
10. Are you simply giving in to life rather than living it?

Your answers to these questions reflect the way you feel about yourself. We want you to give yourself permission to pursue a way which would make you feel good about yourself.

After utilizing many personality theories, we have come to the conclusion that Transactional Analysis offers a concept that is vital to the fulfilled life. Finding the good life comes from being in a position where you can say "I'm okay, you're okay."

Being okay is:

1. I can make a mistake without punishing myself for it.
2. I can give myself credit for a job well done.
3. I can get my needs met.
4. I can feel free to meet the needs of others.
5. I can be open and honest without personal fear.

6. I can evaluate reality in making decisions.
7. I can change if necessary.
8. I can give myself permission to be me.
9. I can accept others without being defensive.
10. I can be a winner!

And you can, really! That's what the next chapters are all about. But before you leave this chapter, settle comfortably in your chair. Relax and let your thoughts wander. Don't resist, fight or be defensive. Now ask yourself:

1. What period of my life was the loneliest?
2. What was the most unforgettable thing that ever happened in my life?
3. If you could have any three people you wanted with you right now, who would they be?

Continue to explore yourself. Ask yourself:

1. What is my biggest success in life?
2. What is my biggest failure?
3. What is my weakest attribute?
4. What is there about my life that I most want to change?
5. Am I an honest person?

Write your answers on paper. Look them over. How do they make you feel? Keep your answers close at hand as you will want to refer to them again.

2

WHAT IS
TRANSACTIONAL
ANALYSIS?

WHAT IS TRANSACTIONAL ANALYSIS?

"An Overview"

Transactional Analysis (T.A.) is a common sense approach to the study of people and their transactions with one another.

It all started with a man by the name of Eric Berne. As a psychiatrist, Dr. Berne was trained in psychoanalysis. His brilliance and determination brought forth a new approach to psychotherapy called transactional analysis.

In the mid 50's a small group of people (therapists, social workers etc.) met at Dr. Berne's home every Tuesday evening. One of the purposes of the first group seminars centered around answers to the social unrest.

"Intimacy" seemed to be one of the most important issues. How can people learn to be intimate?

As the seminars grew it became necessary to incorporate into a non-profit organization. Finally, in 1964, the Internation Transactional Analysis Association was born. (I.T.A.A.) From the research of this organization has come much progress. Today, T.A. is a full grown approach to understanding people and their communication styles. Although T.A. can be a highly complex and sophisticated model for therapy, to the layman, it is simple, workable and what's more—it makes sense.

The specific goal of T.A. is to produce winners. Ther term "winner" is not to be compared to a competitive frame of reference. Rather, a "winner" is one who has decided to maximize his own potential and assume a life position of "I'm okay, you're okay."[1] Eric Berne defines good emotional health as the possession of "awareness, spontaneity, and intimacy."[2]

T.A. uses four approaches to understanding behavior:

1. Structural Analysis: Analyzing what is happening within you.
2. Transactional Analysis: Analyzing what is happening between you and other people.
3. Racket and Game Analysis: Analyzing specific transactions that lead to payoffs of bad feelings.
4. Script Analysis: Analyzing your own life plan.

Briefly, let me explain to you what is involved in *structural analysis*. This is a way you can understand you. There are three parts of you. Each

1. Thomas A. Harris, *I'm OK-You're OK* (New York: Harper & Row) 1969.
2. Eric Berne, *Games People Play* (New York: Grove Press) 1964.

part is called an ego state. Eric Berne defined an ego state as "a system of feeling accompanied by a related set of behavior patterns."[3] These three sets are called: Parent (P) Adult (A) Child (C). Dr. Berne descriptively presented the ego states by the use of three circles.[4]

Parent ego state: The Parent is a collection of ideas, attitudes, cultural styles, and behaviors derived from other people (mostly parents) and from the world around us.

Adult ego state: The Adult, sometimes referred to as the "Computer," logically uses information and appraises reality.

Child ego state: The Child is the feeling part of you. Feelings that are natural (joy, anger) come from your Child.

3. Eric Berne, *Transactional Analysis in Psychotherapy* (New York: Grove Press) 1961, pp. 17-43.
4. Eric Berne, *Transactional Analysis In Psychotherapy.*

As you begin to get acquainted with yourself, you will probably enjoy communicating with others more. T.A. helps you do just that.

When people communicate with one another, there is an exchange of *transactions*. This transaction involves a stimulus and a response between the ego states chosen by the individuals involved.

Take yourself for an example. When a friend begins a conversation with you, she is in a specific ego state. You may choose how you wish to respond. Good health is being autonomous and realizing that you have a choice in this matter of relating and communicating. For instance:

1) You may assume a Controlling Parent position.
   "No, I refuse to allow you to do that!"
2) You may choose a Nurturing Parent position.
   "I'm very concerned about you. I will help you through this decision."
3) You may feel that it is best to make an Adult transaction.
   "I'll give you some information that helped me in making a similar decision."
4) Perhaps an Adapted Child position is more comfortable due to the other person or situation.
   To your boss you might respond....
   "I really feel you are more informed than I am on this issue. I'll go along with your wishes."
5) You may choose to respond from your Natural Child.

"I'd like to do it."

"It sounds like fun."

The words "autonomy" and "choice" are key words to improving your communication.

Why not assume these goals for yourself: 1) To allow yourself to choose the ego state from which you either begin communication or respond in communication. 2) That these choices be the most appropriate and useful to each situation.

In communicating with others, you will find that there are three kinds of transactions.

1) *Complementary*

"Are you going out tonight?" (mother)

"Yes, I'm going to the movie." (daughter)

2) *Crossed*

"Do I need to work overtime tonight?" (secretary)

"All you think about is getting out of work." (boss)

3) *Ulterior* (Duplex)

"Would you meet me at the library to work on our report together?" (male student)

(ulterior) I want to take you out later and get to know you better.

"Sure. I really need to spend sometime looking through some books." (female student)

(ulterior) "I've been wanting you to ask me out for months."

In T.A., transactions such as the previous ones become more understandable through the use of diagrams. For example, the complementary transaction between mother and daughter would be illustrated in the following way:

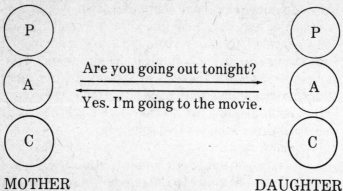

MOTHER   DAUGHTER

(For a further study of this, I would recommend *Transactional Analysis In Brief* by Stanley Woolums, M.D., Michael Brown, Ph. D., and Kristyn Huige, M.A. published by Huron Valley Institute, 3443 Daleview, Ann Arbor, Michigan, 48103.)

At the beginning of this chapter, it was brought to your attention that this whole idea of T.A. began with the need for intimacy. It was reinforced by Berne's definition of health which named intimacy as one of the necessary ingredients.

There is a background to this need for intimacy. It goes back to the basic need in every human being for stimulus-hunger. As a person matures, this need becomes recognition-hunger. A STROKE satisfies part of that hunger. A stroke is a unit of recognition which can be given verbally, non-verbally, or physically. To clarify what is meant by a positive stroke (there are also negative strokes—example: "You look awful today.") the following may be helpful:

1. A smile
2. A wink
3. A handshake
4. A hug
5. Touching
6. Compliments
7. Spending time with someone
8. A simple exchange such as, "Hi! How are you doing?"
9. Praise
10. Gestures and body language that let's you know you are okay or welcomed.

Stroking is necessary for emotional survival. Eric Berne said it so we could all remember it. "Without stroking our spinal cord would shrivel up."[5]

There are healthy ways to get strokes and unhealthy ways. Because there is a need in each of us to structure our time ("structure-hunger") we will go about getting our strokes in specific ways. Those ways depending upon:

1. How I see myself and the world (I'm okay, you're okay).
2. How I have learned to structure my time.
3. The specific stroke that I need at the time.

5. Eric Berne, *The Structure and Dynamics of Organizations & Groups* (Philadelphia: J. B. Lippincott) 1963, p. 157.

A person can structure his time in six ways:

1. Withdrawal (being alone, daydreaming, etc.)
2. Rituals (prayers, exchanges such as, "Good night."—a safe transaction that is predictable)
3. Pastimes (talking about your newest recipe at a P.T.A. social)
4. Activities (working to achieve a goal—planting a garden)
5. Games and Rackets (a potentially dangerous way to structure time and get your strokes)
6. Intimacy (the supreme way to structure time. Trusting—sharing—reaching out—risking—eliminating ulterior transactions and the exploitation of others)

Because games prevent intimacy, T.A. helps you understand them so you can:

1. Realize when you are playing a game.
2. Find out why you are playing a game.
3. Get Adult information about games.
4. Learn to structure your time in a more productive and meaningful way.
5. Learn to get your strokes using honest communication.
6. Make decisions that will take you out of your script and put you into an "I'm okay, you're okay" position.
7. Eliminate your chances of being "hooked" into playing games with others.
8. Enjoy intimacy.
9. Enjoy game-free transactions.
10. Be a winner.

In that games are primary barriers to intimacy, a few explanations are necessary.

Eric Berne defined a game in the book *Games People Play*. "A game is an ongoing series of complementary, ulterior transactions, progressing to a well-defined predictable outcome."[6] He specified that the ulterior aspect and the "pay-off" separated games from procedures, rituals and pastimes. In other words, a game has a hidden message and the result is usually a bad-feeling payoff.

Here is where the term "*racket*" fits into the picture. In an article on "Trading Stamps" by Dr. Berne, he used two words familiar to all of us: 1) Trading Stamps 2) Rackets. The use of street jargon facilitated the understanding of the meaning behind the words.

1. Trading Stamps—The idea of saving up and cashing them in for a prize.
2. Rackets—A scheme—The idea of fraud.

Rackets are described by Berne as having a "currency" known as trading stamps"[7] An example would be as such:

You have worked hard all week to redecorate your home. You are "hurt" because your family has shown you little appreciation for all the time and

6. Eric Berne, *Games People Play*.
7. Eric Berne, ''Trading Stamps.'' Transactional Analysis Bulletin. Vol. 3, 4/64, p. 127.

effort spent. Three consecutive evenings your meals have been eaten with no favorable comment from the family. You feel "hurt." On Saturday evening your husband forgets your anniversary and doesn't even come home. You leave sobbing, catch a plane to mother's house and spend two weeks separated from your family.

You were starving for recognition (strokes) from your family. Rather than communicating this honestly to them, you denied your needs and collected trading stamps (bad feelings). Your racket was hurt. (A racket is a feeling that is exploited as a means of collecting stamps and playing the game.) By the way, we usually have a favorite racket (hurt, anger, confusion) which we choose early in life. Our choice probably came by example from our parents and others or we were stroked for a specific racket.

The concept of psychological games grew in T.A. literature. A specific contribution from Steve Karpman influenced greatly the understanding of games. In his article, "Fairy Tails and Script Drama Analysis," Karpman introduced the element of drama in games. By describing the roles of Persecutor, Rescuer and Victim, he illustrates how dramatically these roles can change while in the midst of a game. Check it out yourself in your own family.

Dad, teen-age daughter Katie and yourself are involved in a dramatic game of "Uproar." Katie has returned home from a date two hours late. Dad meets her at the door with shouts of anger and proceeds to blemish her character.

Dad is the Persecutor.

Katie is the Victim.

You (mother) are the Rescuer.

In the midst of the yelling, you step in and begin to rescue Katie with insulting words to Dad. "How could you treat your daughter like this?" (Dad is now the Victim and you are the Persecutor). Wanting to fight her own battles, Katie jerks you aside with the command, "Mind your own business. Dad is just trying to help me." Here is another switch. Katie is rescuing Dad. You are now the Victim.

This idea of the "switch" was officially incorporated as part of a game by Berne in his book *Sex In Human Loving*.

Someone has to begin the game. A game begins by an initial discount of oneself or the other person. The first move of the game is called a "con." Its psychological message (or "bait"[8] as described by Berne) is disguised by a seemingly okay social message. Quite naturally, the con will be ineffective if there is not a weakness in the other person such as guilt, fear, etc. That weakness is labeled a "gimmick" in T.A. literature.

The last element to complete a game was introduced by Eric Berne in his book *What Do You Say After You Say Hello*. The *grande finale* of the game drama is the crossup. There is a moment of

8. Eric Berne, *Sex In Human Loving* (New York: Simon & Schuster) 1970.

confusion. The players are stunned for a second and wonder, "What happened?"

Now the game formula is complete.

C + G = R S X P (Formula G)

The steps are:

C (Con)	You initiate a game by discounting and hooking into another person's weakness (gimmick)
G (Gimmick)	Other game player feels guilty (if that's his weakness and lets himself get hooked)
R (Response)	There is conversation with an ulterior quality or hidden message
S (Switch)	The roles switch
X (Crossup)	A moment of confusion
P (Payoff)	Bad Feelings—Script has been furthered—Satisfaction of position, structure and stimulus-hunger.

Some people such as Mary Goulding believe that every game does not necessarily have a switch and a crossup. T.A. theorists who hold to this position differentiate between games containing a switch and a crossup and games that do not: Simple games—Games that have a switch and a crossup; Complex Games—Games that do not contain a switch and a crossup.

Although at first glance the steps in a game may

seem lengthy, it must be understood that they could be accomplished in a brief moment.

This leads us into the fourth method used in T.A. to understand human behavior—the *script*. The word alone clarifies the meaning. An actor is handed a script and performs accordingly until the curtain comes down on the final scene.

The script is an individual's life plan. It came about through decisions made in childhood. No doubt his parents influenced his decision.

Script is a negative term, therefore a "winning person" is not considered a scripted person. She is rather operating autonomously.

There are two types of losing scripts:

1) Harmartic Script— A script with a tragic ending
2) Banal Script— A non-winning script which eliminated closeness and intimacy. There is little or no risking.

In the definition of a script, reference is made to "early parental influence." No one can deny the facts that parental figures influence the child. In order for the child to survive, she feels the need to please the big people in her life. She will make decisions accordingly which could initiate and perpetuate a script.

Obviously the parental influence can be either positive or negative. T.A. literature makes the positive and negative distinction as "permissions" and "injunctions." Permission from birth onward allows for self-acceptance and growth. An injunction, though, is a prohibitive message. It is characterized by the word "DON'T," usually sent to the child in non-verbal ways and greatly influences the script decision. It is often a negative form of control that "prohibits" a feeling of okayness as well as the development of emotional health. In most cases, it stems out of a need for a coping mechanism to external problems in the parent's environment.

Robert and Mary Goulding have contributed much to the idea of injunctions. (For further study: Progress in Group and Family Therapy.)

Below is a list of injunctions to facilitate your understanding of what is meant by the term.

1. Don't BE   (Don't exist)
2. Don't FEEL   (Don't be aware of your own sensations)
3. Don't FEEL   (Don't express your own true feelings)
4. Don't be YOU   (male, female, color, culture, etc.)
5. Don't be YOUR AGE   (Don't grow up or don't be a child)
6. Don't BELONG   (...to a family, withdrawal)
7. Don't SUCCEED   (Don't accomplish or make it)
8. Don't THINK   (Discounting what the child does, says, thinks)
9. Don't BE CLOSE (physical and emotional closeness)

10. Don't be WELL OR SANE   (It's easier to be "crazy" than live autonomously)
11. Don't ACT
12. Don't BE IMPORTANT

Permission is the opposite of the injunction. For example, it's okay to be here, to think and solve problems, to feel your true feelings and on down the list.

There are many other areas of T.A. we haven't discussed in this chapter. This simple overview, touching only the crucial areas, will hopefully lay a foundation for you as you read on.

3

A TOUCH OF GRACE

A TOUCH OF GRACE

Ann had a hint of tears in her eyes. Her wrinkled brow and set jaw indicated that she was fighting back a flood of feelings. She rose from her chair and prepared to leave. It was obvious that she wanted to hurry from the room. I could only guess at the need for her hasty departure for the reasons remained locked in her nondisclosed silence.

I watched as she walked away. Her shoulders sagged as if she were laboring under the burden of a ten-ton feather. Why had she left so hurriedly? Our conversation seemed so friendly. I was left to guess and not to know.

My job is to know people—to open the hidden secrets and untapped reservoirs of their inner life. Sometimes it is a difficult job. It is made difficult because people are afraid to reveal themselves. In reality, we can never know another person unless they choose to disclose their private thoughts and feelings to us. Sometimes people are afraid to disclose what they feel.

Ann is such a person. I did not know why she could not share with me, but there are many Anns. I have seen those same set jaws and sagging shoulders in churches, at parties, and walking down the street. Some inner part within me always cries a little. You know—those sad, disquieting and silent tears that senses pain hidden behind a smiling face and false facade of body language. Inner secrets, walled in brick by brick, designed and constructed by reasonable and logical defenses.

A person like Ann needs to be touched. Ann needs to touch. I am not talking only about physical touch. I am referring to a form of communication that spans the chasm between two people.

Touching is what this chapter is all about. A simple example of touching is the realization of the existence of another person. A more complex definition of touching is love.

Love is hard to define because it involves almost all the feelings that a person is capable of experiencing.

Let me illustrate. Recall with me the first time your heart's heart touched another person. A transformation took place. Suddenly you liked to walk in the rain while only yesterday you resented getting wet. You didn't notice the patches of grey clouds, only the rich and quickening blue skies surrounding them. A stirring sense of expectation and excitement filled your life. You were touched.

Recall again your mountaintop experiences with God. You received a sense of well-being. You experienced people and life in a new way. You even loved the grouchy waitress when she brought you burnt toast. You "stopped to hear a robin sing" and praise slid easily from your lips. Your soul sang "He touched me."

Love begins with touching. Love is our highest aim, but probably our most illusive endeavor.

Love does have a beginning and an end. The beginning is when the infant is first comforted by a caring parent's soothing voice and tender caresses. Love ends in the culminating awareness that I am cared for by God, others and myself.

The gap of time between the first caress and the certainty of caring depends on the multiple experiences of touching and being touched.

Let us illustrate the importance of touching. There is an outstanding book called *The First Year of Life* by Dr. Renee Spitz. It is about living, precious human beings at the start of life—their first year.

In his book, Dr. Spitz described these children as receiving minimal human contacts in their first year. After all, who can resist the cooing attraction of a new born child? But these were institutional children—young lives without a caring mother to give them instant attention. The children were cared for as far as food, cleanliness and the necessities of life were concerned. Only one thing was missing: there was no adoring adult to pick them up and tenderly nestle them in loving arms. Can you imagine the results? Most of them died early in life. Yes they died, even though there was no apparent reason for their death. And Dr. Spitz's research has been documented many times.

The infants died because they did not receive the necessary ingredient for survival—loving strokes.

We are born with certain drives and needs. One such drive is the physical need for food and water. Without them we would die. We are also born with a psychological need—a hunger for touching. You notice I used the word hunger. Do you recall the beatitude which says that "Blessed are those that hunger and thirst." We have as much a hunger for touching as we do for food. Believe me it's true. I have seen too many love starved people to doubt it.

Let us make what may seem like a dramatic statement: The single greatest cause of all problems is the failure of the person to touch or be touched.

For years both of us have taught at various schools, seminars and workshops. The single most oft-quoted statement is, "I feel unloved."

Why should this be? We know we cannot live without love. Why should it be so hard to love. Let us again suggest a reason: We have not learned to touch and we have learned to be afraid of touching.

Please, do not make the mistake of assuming that touching simply means physically touching another person. It means giving recognition to the existence of someone else. We can sometimes do this by a word, a gesture or even a frown. Any form of communication that conveys the recognition that the other person exists is touching.

We spoke briefly about the need for touching. We

said that the infant cannot survive without it. You know, this is equally true for adults. Oh yes, you can go on living, perhaps repeating the same mundane, boring manner of life, but you are not living, you are only existing.

Today you can make some choices which will change your life from a mere existence to a fulfilling satisfied person. There are several things you must do, however:

1. Realize you have a problem.
2. Make a choice you are going to do something about it.
3. Seek ways of making positive changes in your life.
4. Refuse to settle for living a second rate life.
5. Accept your strengths and depend on them.
6. Tolerate mistakes without putting yourself down for them.
7. Accept the reality of situations you cannot change.
8. Seriously attempt to be aware of yourself and others.
9. Listen—don't just hear what is being said to you.
10. Be open and honest.

Some of you may be saying, "Okay, I've tried all those things you suggested and I still feel unfulfilled." We may be talking about problems involved in touching.

In the introduction of the book we said that almost everything we know, feel or sense is taken from other people. That's true—the "Big People" in our early life, shape, mold and to a large extent determine how we feel about touching or being touched. From them, we learn basic feelings such as love, fear, hate, anger, joy and all the feelings of life.

We are thinking of not just one but many women who come to us and say, "I wish my husband would just hold me, but I know every time he hugs me it leads to sex."

Another example is a man who says, "My wife wants me to support her but she doesn't want to give me the support I need."

Another person may say "I know God answers prayers for others, but he doesn't seem to answer mine."

These, and many others, are examples of the fear of touching.

This fear is a learned response developed in childhood and reinforced throughout life. Usually, underlying a reluctance for touching is a fear. The fear may be developed through misinformation received as a child.

For example, in our society men have been taught it is not proper to cry. Yet one of the clearest evidences of a person being touched by someone else may be his tears.

Sometimes you may want to say something very nice to another person, but you have a fear of not being understood. You feel blocked in reaching out to that person. You may even want to say something nice to yourself but that would be bragging or having too much pride. You are scripted as to what to say and when to say it. Sometimes the kindest feelings go unexpressed leaving a feeling of insensitivity and indifference in its wake.

This happens in many marriages. Two people may really love each other but fail to touch each other with gentle words and tender caresses. Is the answer simply they are insensitive to each other? Not always—they are quite often afraid to reach out verbally or physically because they run the risk of rejection.

A woman recently told us that she is comfortable in her aloneness. She said that every time she reaches out, she gets hurt. Well, the truth of the matter is she is continually hurting. Much of the money she makes is spent on a variety of doctors treating physical symptoms which stem from her self-imposed state of alienation. Her spine is shriveled because she is not receiving the necessary strokes for personal satisfaction.

Right now ask yourself the following questions. Be honest and open. You have nothing to lose and perhaps much to gain.

1. Can I openly express myself to at least one other person?
2. Do I freely accept what someone else has to say without criticizing him?
3. Do I receive the affection that I have a right to receive?
4. Am I afraid to express my deeper thoughts?
5. How many people do I trust?

6. If I died tomorrow who would really care?
7. Am I loved or just used by others?
8. Am I really capable of deep love?
9. Is this life a rotten place?
10. Can I make choices about my dependency on others?

If you feel from answering these questions that a problem exists, then your next question is "What do I do about it?"

Stating a problem is sometimes easier than finding a solution. Part of finding any answer to a problem involves believing that an answer exists.

I am reminded of a young man who stopped me one day, asked if I were a psychologist and said he wanted to talk to me. We arranged a time and place to meet and discuss whatever his inquiry concerned.

I remember well our first and only meeting. He spent forty-five minutes telling me his story. Actually, his problems were not severe and there were many possible answers. When I suggested some alternatives, he immediately told me he had tried them and they didn't work. When I finally suggested he did not believe an answer existed, he started to leave. Still with me? Do you hear what he was really saying underneath? He didn't believe an answer existed!

I recall a warm, vibrant man of God who always responded to a problem by saying "Well, let's see which of God's answers are correct for your problem."

Believe there is an answer and then act upon that belief.

We stated that almost all problems center around touching.

Examine your life, your precious God-given life, and find areas where you are not able to reach out and touch someone. Let's restate that—examine the areas of your life where you will not allow yourself to be touched. That's a problem area.

With some embarrassment and a lot of courage I am going to relate a personal example. Recently Marjorie and I had a chance to meet Bob Newhart, the well-known TV personality. Marjorie was excited and showed it. She was bubbly, jazzed and honest in her enthusiasm. I was somewhat reserved, cool and could not fully appreciate her feelings. When the time came to meet the "great" man, her excitement was doubled; my lack of interest was diminished. In fact, I thought she was acting rather childish. She asked if she could get his autograph. I replied, "Get his shoe size if you want to." Frankly, I was feeling slightly superior. Here I was with a Ph.D., vast knowledge of human behavior, a successful person. Why should I condescend to following after a mere entertainer's signature.

The next day I was telling a friend of mine, a man I respect very much, that we had met Bob Newhart. He responded with "Wow, wish I could have gotten his autograph." Then it struck me. I was protecting myself from being touched by the excitement by my own need to elevate my abilities and accomplishments above someone else. Perhaps I relate to attempting to be everyone's big Daddy. I couldn't let my "free kid" out enough. Do any of you men suffer from this kind of problem?

Some of you may say "Well, I came from a family where people never really touched each other."

Do you mean, you never physically touched each other or do you mean you never emotionally touched each other? I assume you mean the latter. There is a difference, a real difference.

Let us suggest an alternative for you. If your reason for lack of closeness is "I never learned to be emotionally close" then do the following things for one week:

1. Take a person, any person, and try to get to really know them. In other words, play psychologist.
2. Share a secret experience of yours with someone you trust. I know that's risky, but try it.
3. Look for an area in your life which is hard to do and try doing it. Perhaps with only one person or maybe more.
4. Hug at least five close friends when you greet them.
5. Ask God to give you courage and believe he has.
6. Tell yourself I am going to be nice to me by doing something neat, just for me.
7. When you are in conversation with someone else, attempt to concentrate on what that

person is saying. This means forgetting yourself and listening to the other person.

Closeness involves many attitudes. Some attitudes prevent closeness. Those attitudes may be:

1. Prejudging a situation.

   "I already know how others see me." If you meet me tomorrow, please let me judge whether or not I am going to like you, don't do it for me. I may discover in you the ingredients for a best friend.

2. Prejudging another person.

   "He's a psychologist, he only wants to analyze me." No, I want to know you. I am just like you. I need to be touched, cared for, recognized. Everyone has the same need—the hunger for positive strokes.

3. Prejudging yourself.

   "It just isn't me. I can't talk to people."

   Change the word *can't* to *won't*. you can make choices. You can change. Why? Because underlying all behavior is a need for positive recognition from God, others and self. Perhaps the "image of God" may be related to a need for touching.

Suppose for example that you were not endowed by birth with a hunger for touching. Probably, the Mother's touch or soft words would have no impact upon your life. You could grow up to be a machine or animal that only needs to have their basic physical needs met. Touching and being touched is a necessary condition of life.

Positive attitudes toward touching involve:
1. Accept the reality of your need.

   You must have your needs met. Your need for a relationship with God is primary. I once had a woman tell me "I may be loused up emotionally, but I have a relationship with God. I would rather be a Christian with a lot of problems than be the most well-adjusted non-Christian.

   We also have a need for others. Can you imagine spending the rest of your life without ever talking to another human being?

   When I worked at a prison some years ago, I saw several men who had been in solitary confinement for only a few days. They were disoriented, confused and irrational. They needed contact with others.
2. Look at what you are already doing well in your relationships. Continue to practice it and expand on it.
3. Genuinely praise others and yourself. Don't be afraid to say "Honey, that's a good job," or "I really enjoyed that dinner." Sometimes you may want to say to yourself, "Hey, I did that well."

   Praise is mentioned more in scripture than any other concept. It works. If you are doing it, continue.
4. Be good to yourself.

   The Bible teaches us to love other people. It does not say love others, hate yourself.

Sometimes Christians feel they are being "spiritual" by self-denial and personal castigation.

All ten (commandments) are wrapped up in this one, to love your neighbor as you love yourself. Romans 13:9, The Living Bible.

What Paul is saying here is that *all* Commandments are summed up in this one.

You must love yourself. Treat yourself with the same respect, consideration and even forgiveness you treat another person you love very much. This is the basis for touching the inner parts of your own self.

5. Thank God for the fact he has made you a person who can choose, decide and have alternatives in life.

Of all the creatures that are created, only you can make choices. You may say, "Well, I really can't make many choices." Yes, you can. God has given you that resource. Again, always try to change the word "can't" to "won't."

"Can't" leaves you powerless, at the mercy of forces beyond your control. God gives you a way out. If you are living a life you don't like, you can choose to live differently. Why? Because you have the ability from God to make a choice.

51

6. Feel good about your ability to love.

Yes, you have that ability. It may be hard to do, but you have that ability. How did you get it? Well, someone, somewhere and at some time reached out to you in love. That was the beginning. You experienced it. Now you can reach out to someone else.

7. Remember you have been loved.

Again you have had experiences of being loved. you may not have felt it at the time but you were loved. In fact, you are being loved right now. I don't know what other human is loving you but God certainly is. Claim that—it will make you feel better.

Why should you feel better abut yourself? Because all of life yearns to express itself through you. You are a unique, highly complex and adored creation of the Master's hand. Hidden beneath the uncertainties, doubts and fears of life resides a beauty and gentility unequaled in all of nature. You are, you exist, you have meaning. Share and be shared. Open yourself to be vulnerable to others and you will discover the unimaginable qualities of goodness and life within you.

"Blessed are those that touch for they will be touched!"

4

THE GREAT DISCOUNT

THE GREAT DISCOUNT

"I hurt, oh how I hurt. Daddy, please do something." The words, almost whispered instead of spoken, tore at his heart. His 16-year-old daughter was dying. She was in great pain. He pondered, how can this be? Can't I do something? He couldn't and she died.

This short paragraph is taken from a real life drama of a friend of ours. His daughter, in the flower of her youth with the vast expanse of unrealized expectations and dreams before her, contracted a fatal illness.

Our friend is a fine, mature and well educated person. Yet he wondered how this could happen to him. Yes, he knew it happened to others. He had friends who had gone through personal tragedy. But now it happened to him and he felt angry, hurt and confused.

In other words, he felt almost totally discounted.

In our last chapter we spoke of discounts and how it feels to experience the pain of nonrecognition.

Even in losing a loved one we feel discounted. The feeling may be that the loved one has left us, neglected us or gone away. The relationship has been severed, the precious ties of connectiveness cut and the life force of mutual love and caring lost. The above is an extreme example of a person's feeling of personal loss and tragedy, but there are so many other ways of experiencing the same feelings at lesser but still important degrees.

Imagine for a moment that you're walking down the street and you spot someone you haven't seen for several months. You call their name and wave. There's no reply on their part. Instead, they keep walking on nervously without a nod in your direction. How would you feel?

Or, how many times have you prayed repeatedly for a specific request and apparently received no answers. How do you feel?

Or, the day has been long and tiring. You're anxious to be home and see your family. When you walk in the door you're greeted with a cool "hello." How do you feel?

These are examples of feeling *discounted*. At this moment you're relating to these situations in that you've probably had many such unpleasant experiences also.

What does it mean to discount or be discounted? It essentially means a loss of self-worth or being minimized. Muriel James defines a discount in her book as, "the lack of attention or negative attention that hurts emotionally or physically."

What we are saying is that you have a feeling of being ignored. Words are spoken, gestures implied or situations occur in which your sense of self-worth is diminished.

Discounting seems to stem from a very common yet universal experience called denial. We can discount ourselves and others in many ways, such as:

1. *Denial of Your Self-worth.*

   Several years ago a lovely young lady came to see us. It was only a matter of minutes and she was in tears. Through the sobs we learned that she had been married less than five years. She loved her husband, but the story revealed that her needs had not been met in even the simplest ways. She had suffered harsh treatment and abuse. In the midst of her explanation, she looked up at us, dabbed her eyes and said,"I've never done anything about this problem because I'm a good Christian wife!" This well intended woman had denied herself the right to self-expression which is an integral part of self-worth.

2. *Denial of Your Individuality.*

   Our own individuality involves such things as: (1) Making our own choices. (2) Entertaining alternatives. (3) Making decisions that are mutually beneficial to ourselves and others. Some psychologists have indicated in the past that there is a difference between neurotic and healthy dependency. Neurotic dependency is when a person is unable to make decisions for themselves. We know of a man who is very successful in business. Although he has the ability to think and make valid judgments, he discounts himself and his abilities to make decisions at home. His wife is always the final word.

3. *Denial of "Me"—The Person.*

We were speaking one evening on the subject of communication. After the workshop a lady came up and introduced herself to us. I remember her words, "Hello there, I'm the President's wife." We exchanged a greeting. I reached my hand for hers and asked, "What is your name?" She replied similarly, only this time she stated her husband's name. "John Doe, the President of our organization. I'm his wife." By this time I had gently started to shake her hand. I softly repeated my question, "What is *your* name?" Nervously, as though to say it's not too important, she said, "I'm Mrs. Doe." By this time I had a twinkle in my eye and a mischievous grin on my face. "What's your name?" I inquired for one last time. This time it worked. Her eyes lit up with awareness and she squealed out with all kinds of delight, "I'm Susan!" This was an insightful moment in Susan's life. She felt what it was like to experience Susan, the person, without discounting herself.

4. *Denial of My Needs*

Do you remember in the first chapter we mentioned how people often deny their needs. In fact, we said that in our experience, Christians often act as though needs should be denied. More than likely, if they were questioned on the issue, they would agree that we all have needs and that those needs should be met. Yet, it always seems that these needs are expressed in such a web of apologies that they become confused with irrelevant wants or selfish passion. It always amazes us to see and experience how rapidly a person can convince himself that his needs are the unworthy requests of an ungrateful servant. Believe it or not, they even attempt to convince us.

Let us give you an illustration that occurs several times a week. Try to fantasize this in your mind so you can feel the impact of what is happening.

A gentlemen comes in to see us in total desperation. He is broken in spirit, perhaps literally sobbing tears and obviously out of control. We spend time with him. Finally, he feels safe and he begins to share how depressed he really is. He concludes by making a statement such as this: "I don't know what's wrong with me. I can't understand why I'm the way I am." After a few moments of dialogue, we're aware that this man has little or no love, relatively no security and seemingly no one with whom to talk.

He knows he is feeling hopeless, depressed and alone. But he insists there is no reason for his condition. We know there are reasons for his condition. The reality is that he needs to be nurtured, loved and cared for by others. The healing will only be realized if he allows himself to accept his needs rather than discounting them.

5. *Denial of My Need for Others.*

Do you really need others? You will say "Of course I do, you know that." We would challenge you to carefully reflect on this question. Sometimes we can know something but our behavior may indicate that we do not put that knowing into action.

Many people who come to see us express specifically that they have a need for social contacts. They want to be with others and experience all the advantages that come from warm interpersonal relationships. However, they offer many reasons why they cannot fulfill their needs for others.

For example, a young, attractive woman we know has a job, good health and much independence. She is free to select whatever social activities she wants. The example sounds pretty good so far doesn't it? After all, having personal freedom is a very desirable choice. But what price do we pay for this kind of freedom? Some forms of freedom bring a subtle form of bondage. She may be free to choose what she will do, where she will go and when she will do it. She is not free, however, to choose the kind and quality of feelings she will have.

Strange but true, one feeling may mask a deeper need. In the young woman's case she is very angry with men. She, perhaps unconsciously, looks for flaws in every man she meets. Even with other women, she projects feelings of anger, unfairness, and pride. Basically she has a need for tender, warm and satisfying relationships with others, but she denies this need by finding some fault with others which inhibits any significant relationship with them.

We have been discussing the subject of discounting. Frankly, we have to say there is no positive benefit psychologically or spiritually when you are in the process of discounting. By definition, a discount is a minimizing of the person, his worth, esteem and potential for growth.

We have been taught that a "man is not to think more highly of himself than he ought to think." Some Christians take pride in the feeling, "I really do not like myself." They say, "The important thing is that God loves me." On the surface these are true statements. However, many problems are handled by the misapplications of specific truths to general situations.

In the past the "good" Christian was characterized as spiritual because he spoke about how bad he was, looked rejected and accepted his problems as an inevitable consequence of being alive. Most transactions that are not direct and honest produce disastrous results. The "good" Christian is really saying, "Look how spiritual I am, I really know how bad I am." If that person were to feel good about himself, he would probably apologize and then feel guilty.

By this time we hope you are convinced that you have a right to feel good about yourself. Here are some suggestions that will help you to feel better about you.

1. Make a list of everything that you find good about yourself.
2. Accept the positive strokes that other people give you.
3. Starting today—first thing in the morning look in the mirror and tell yourself "I love you" three times.
4. Treat yourself with the same consideration you would another person you love very deeply.
5. Every day thank God he created you.
6. Today accept your own uniqueness—you have talents and abilities no one else has.
7. Accept the fact God created you and he does not make mistakes.

8. Take an interest in your own good health and appearance.
9. Use more energy on nurturing yourself than criticizing yourself.
10. Do one good thing just for you—today.

Perhaps, at this point you are feeling good about yourself. You have hope because there are steps you can take which will enhance your self-worth and curb discounting.

Recently we talked to a couple whose marriage was being torn apart by inconsideration and insensitivity. The wife knew the marriage could not continue unless something was done. Reluctantly, the husband agreed to come see us. He appeared friendly, smiled broadly and stated he "had no need to be here."

One of his opening questions to us was, "Do you have any problems?" When we agreed that everyone has problems, he felt we could not be of any help to him. Of course, with that expectation, there was no one he could see who could help him.

There is a direct relationship between the inability to solve a problem and discounting. In order to clarify this statement we would like to use the four levels of discounting as stated by Jacqui Schiff in her articles on Passivity.[9] These levels are:
(1) Discounting the problem
(2) Discounting the importance of the problem
(3) Discounting the solvability of the problem

9. Jacqui Schiff, Cathexis Reader (New York: Harper & Row) p. 15.

(4) Discounting the self

These points could be illustrated with Mr. X, a young man with a lovely wife, good children and a bright future. He came to see us because he could not seem to feel good about himself. The first session quickly revealed that he was very angry with his father who had abused, ignored and damaged him. When confronted with, "You appear to be very angry with your parents," he denied it. To him, this was not the problem. It was only that he was unhappy. He was discounting the problem.

Discounting the problem is the most severe. Total denial eliminates any responsibility for action. When someone comes to our office in a crisis, the chances are fairly high that days, months or even years of discounting the problem have existed. Only the crisis jars the individual into facing the existing need.

Later, in another session, he insightfully realized he was angry. However, he stated, "What's the use, you can't do anything about it anyway." Second and third phases together—discounting both the importance and solvability of the problem.

Finally, he ran the spectrum by saying, "I don't have a right to be angry anyway." Now he was discounting himself.

Here are some suggestions for meeting the demands that problems create:

1. Realize that when your life is not functioning smoothly, there is probably some personal problem present.

2. Do not minimize the importance of any problem you may have.
3. Realize that you have God given abilities to cope with stress.
4. If you are faced with indecision, ask someone to help you.
5. When there is an apparent problem, face it from an okay position.
6. Realize that you are a person with a problem, not a problem person.
7. Assume there is always a solution.
8. Confine the problem within limits without letting it dominate your entire personality.
9. Don't make the problem bigger than it is.
10. When you find yourself saying, "I can't," change that to "I won't."
11. Accept the resources that God has given you.
12. Make an expectation of yours, that with God's help the problem can be handled.
13. Follow the examples of Jesus through his problem solving.
14. Love yourself in spite of the problem.
15. Seek to find more information on the problem.

You may be curious as to why we have not mentioned "the power of God." We believe in the power of God, having witnessed many manifestations of it in our own personal lives. Frankly, we feel that people sometimes discount the importance of their problems and themselves by saying, "Let God take care of it." On the surface, this sounds like a profound and mature Christian point of view. On the social level, he is saying, "Let God take care of it, but on the psychological level he is saying, "I don't want to face it!" The consequences of such an attitude will most likely be unfortunate. Our problem may go unsolved and then we may feel neglected by God. As a result, God appears to be an uncaring Father and we continue in our not-okay position.

In His love for His children, God has given us resources and abilities. His plan of Grace is based on our sharing and caring for one another. By stating, "My problem is too big for me, God will have to handle it"—we are discounting God's plan for us as well as our own abilities.

If we as Christians cannot depend on what our resources and what we can become, then our spiritual relationship is of little value.

The Kingdom of Heaven is the kingdom of "right relationships" with God, others and self.

5

THE FERTILE SOIL

THE FERTILE SOIL

"And He spake many things to them in parables, saying, Behold, a sower went out to sow. And when he sowed, some seeds fell beside the road, and the birds came and devoured them. Some fell on rocky places, where they did not have much soil; and immediately they sprung up, because they had no depth of soil. But when the sun had risen, they were scorched; and because they had no root, they withered away. And others fell among the thorns, and the thorns came and choked them out. And others fell on good soil and yielded a crop . . ."

This is a familiar portion of Scripture, I'm sure. I remember hearing this story as a child in Sunday School. My teacher brought cups of soil to the classroom and each one of us planted our seeds. We watched them grow, and finally took our plant home to Mother. I remember how proud I was to have had a part in helping something to grow. I don't remember, however, any moral or reason for the story that had been told to us in class.

As the years went by, this parable came up time and time again in church. I heard it taught and preached with great enthusiasm. The meanings and theological interpretations were usually quite similar and always made sense.

It wasn't until about a year ago or so that this parable began to jell for me in a new way. Because the following ideas are so terribly meaningful to me, I'm going to give you some background. Here's how it all started and developed.

In my book, *Getting to Know You*, I made several references to my years as an elementary school teacher. It takes very little sensitivity to pick up the spark of enthusiasm in my words about teaching. There's nothing like it that I've ever experienced. A teacher has the privilege of motivating human beings to grow physically, mentally, emotionally and spiritually.

As of late, the majority of my teaching experience has been in the college classroom. In any classroom however, (whether children or adults) an area of concern kept creeping up. Let me say it like it is. I always seemed to face one gigantic barrier:

Not reading problems.

Not poor spelling.

Not discipline.

Not boredom.

These problems I can handle. With a little innovation and a lot of motivation, a teacher can push her students over these hurdles.

The barrier I'm particularly concerned about is

the total lack of self-worth on the part of individual students. Should a teacher be faced with an, "I'm not okay" philosophy collectively expressed by a number of students in one class, she is likewise faced with frustration and discouragement. And let me tell you, that's scary. These students become part of your life four to nine months out of a year. They are part of you and you cannot hide from that "feeling" of responsibility, that desire to nurture, that emotion of compassion, that challenge to create, that sense of attachment and belonging.

So easily, however, those earthy, human passions are seemingly blocked by a sturdy wall surrounding a frightened, insecure individual. The graffiti is easily visible:

I'm scared.

I can't trust you.

I can think.

I've never experienced caring.

I'm afraid to be me.

I'll probably fail.

It's no use.

I'm lonely.

I've got to get attention one way or another.

I'm not okay.

Every new semester I face this problem. There is a difference between elementary children and college students. The difference is obvious. Those little ones are still open and the hurts have not been so compounded by the years.

I mentioned to you earlier how the parable of the

soil took on new personal meaning for me about a year or so ago.

I was asked to speak at a workshop sponsored by the National Educator's Fellowship. Being so heavily involved in education myself, I was honored to have an opportunity to share with others in the field.

My subject was to be on "Education in the Media." Since I had appeared on radio and T.V. quite often, the leaders were hoping I might relate what is presently being done in the area. There were many startling statistics for me to give them. I could dazzle them with future prospects of education and the media. After all, I was there to entertain, excite and challenge these teachers!

The workshop was at Arrowhead Springs. The day was crisp and clear. I pulled up to the meeting room and began to unload my visual aids and teaching tools. Another workshop was in session so I walked around the quiet, peaceful grounds of the conference area.

Then, as though I saw it written in the sky (I didn't, by the way) some new thoughts came to me. Thoughts that not only changed my seminar outline, but turned my thinking around. I saw myself as a person, as a teacher and as a mother in a different position. My information, skills, methods and goals fell into proper perspective. My role as a Christian mother, a Christian teacher and as me—a person in the community—seemed far more specific than ever before. Let me go further and say that these at last felt right. Congruency is the feeling I'm talking about. My role or responsibility in these areas now appeared to be obtainable. I could grasp on to something that felt right and worthy.

Perhaps it was an attitude I picked up at the conference when I first arrived. I spoke to some of the teachers and administrators. I picked up a program and checked out what had been covered. I peeked in on some of the workshops. I overheard some of the conversations. Whatever it was, I sensed it and it clarified my thinking. There seemed to be prevalent a feeling of failure and despair.

1. How can we teach morals to our youth?
2. Why can't we get discipline any more?
3. Do our children understand honor and morality today?
4. Are we allowed to expose them to the religions of the world, or are we tied down to total secularism?
5. How do we expose children to beauty, and to God and all His benefits?

These were the questions being asked. They were questions I had asked before. What was really being said was:

1. We can't seem to teach morals and goodness to our children anymore.
2. Children are not submitting to discipline.
3. Children are rejecting honor and morality as we present it.
4. We feel legally bound to secularism. Exposing

73

children to religion and other cultures seems to be risky.

5. We have failed in our attempts to show beauty and God's benefits to our youth.

I could not go in that workshop and talk for an hour on the mass media. What good is a television lesson or any other lesson if the recipients aren't prepared?

This is how it all came together. This is when the problem seemed to have a reasonable solution. God's remedy was there all along, but it hadn't made sense until now.

The mother, father, teacher, helper, minister who cultivates the soil of an individual can honestly say his life is worthwhile. No more despair, but instead, hope. No longer do I feel constraint or failure, I experience winning. In my winning, I am producing and promoting other winners.

Irrespective of your primary interpretation of this Scripture, I am suggesting that the soil can represent a healthy, secure, autonomous personality who views life from an "okay" position.

As we stated earlier, Eric Berne labels a healthy person as one who has achieved autonomy. Autonomy is achieved as one maximizes his potential for awareness, intimacy and spontaneity.

As a parent or as a teacher, can't you see the challenge of promoting these three areas in the lives of students, loved ones and friends?

I am suggesting to you that fertile soil is the foundation upon which truth is built. Its minerals are intimacy, spontaneity and awareness. Its label is autonomy.

How can you develop such characteristics in yourself and in others?

We would like to think that your attitude would be that of hope. If you have encouraged a child or another human being to accept his own self-worth, you have performed a worthy task. You have helped to break down the wall that blocks learning. You have begun building a bridge of communication which connects people and cultures.

There are attitudes that you can accept and steps you can take to help cultivate fertile soil.

1. *Accept a Person Where He Is.*

I sat quietly in a room with a grieving woman. Her husband was gone, and all that seemed to remain were debts, unfinished business and loneliness. She wept. Through her tears emerged anger. He had left her and she screamed out how much she hated him for it. The outburst continued as she turned on me. "You will never see me at church again," she cried. "Never! If God is in control, then why did He take my husband?"

That day . . . that hour was certainly not the time to admonish. There was no need to defend against her anger. All the inspirational jargon that came to mind could not have comforted her.

I accepted her as she was. She was in terrible pain from grief. She was frightened. She was alone. I could not make the pain go away. Neither

75

did I expect or try to stop her from grieving. She was at that place and she needed to be there.

Her last words to me when she left still act as a reminder to me of this point. "Thank you, thank you, all my friends ever tell me is to stop crying. It felt good," she continued, "to get it out!"

2. *Make No Judgment About His Present Condition.*
When we were at a conference a story was told to us that illustrates this point well. The person sharing the story with us was speaking of herself. We'll write it as it was spoken to us:

"Years ago I was desperately in love with a man. We were inseparable. For several years we lived together although we had not been legally married.

"I was not feeling well and there seemed to be several minor physical things wrong with me. I felt down emotionally because I was not working and living at maximum potential.

"At the same time, I became interested in going to church, and had several books about Christianity that seemed to be directing me toward faith in Christ. I began to share the ideas with the man I loved so much. He also became curious as well as excited about the Lord. One day we decided to go and talk to a minister. There were two reasons: (1) I wanted to get back on my feet emotionally and physically. (2) We were honestly seeking God, but had many questions.

"We walked into the pastor's study. We sat

down and introduced ourselves. I spoke first by giving my name and then introduced my friend by giving his name. The pastor said, 'Are you married?' We both shook our heads in the negative. 'Are you living together?' he continued to question. 'We have lived together for three years,' I immediately replied.

"Then it happened. The minister turned and looked directly into the eyes of the dearest person in my life and said, 'Sir, you have sinned! It is your sin that has caused this woman to be ill. Right now, this moment, I want you to say that you will move out and never see her again.'

"I got angry but he sat motionless. Quietly, he patted my hand as if to tell me to cool down. Then he spoke—softly as though to assure himself of control, 'I came here seeking God, but you judged me before I had a chance. Will God do the same thing?' Then he grabbed my arm and we left."

3. *See Him As a Maximized Person.*

Only yesterday I hosted a television show called Unit V. The name signifies that for five years a unit of people have presented needs of the community to the television audience. The subject was "Crisis in Education." One of the guests was a vivacious high school teacher by the name of Cassandra McMillon. Cassandra was from the black community, and from the moment we introduced ourselves we knew we were destined to be friends. We had only a few minutes before the taping was to begin. "Well, Cassandra, we're supposed to talk about Crisis in Education," I affirmed. As I slid into the make-up chair, I prodded her a little, "What turns you on about this subject? You know what I'm after," I continued, "What is it about education that really gets to you?" One of the broadest smiles I think I have ever seen came across her face, and I knew we had a great program coming. With a twinkle in her eyes, she teased me, "I bet you think I want to talk about busing, don't you? Well, there's something much more urgent that needs to be said," she assured me. She went on to tell a story about herself that made me proud to be a human being and a member of the educational profession. I'll write it as she told it.

"Several years ago I was trained and ready to teach school. I had applied to teach in the Los Angeles schools but there were no vacancies. I have always been a teacher. I was born to teach.

"There was a terrible riot this particular morning in one of our schools. The young people had guns, knives and who knows what else. I called the school, gave them my name and told them that I could help them. I proceeded to explain myself. I told them that I knew many of these children from camp work. I could go in and talk to them and they would listen to me. Naturally the school welcomed me but cautioned me as to the danger involved.

"I did exactly what I said I would. I walked into the school, spoke to the kids and shortly after, the horrifying event was over."

As Cassandra finished her story, I was dazed with admiration for her courage. "Cassandra," I questioned, "What's your secret?" She straightened her shoulder and pointed her finger at me and said, "I saw those kids as healthy, productive young men and women. I expected change." "By the way," she added, "I couldn't have done this had I not felt okay about me!"

Cassandra is a living illustration of a courageous woman willing to see a person as a maximized human being.

4. *Provide an Atmosphere of Comfort.*

This is an extremely important point because anyone can do it. Anyone can create a climate of comfort, security and serenity. You don't have to have a fancy office. You don't even have to be alone. Even in a crowded room, you can create climate. Through your sensitivity, your voice, your body language, you can allow a person to feel safe.

I had this idea confirmed to me about a year ago. I came into my office late in the afternoon and met one of my former clients leaving the office. My face must have showed my surprise, "Did you come in to make an appointment?" I questioned. She gave me a big hug and said, "I just came in and sat in your office. Things have been hectic and confused lately. I need just to sit and think in a safe, comfortable place." "It worked," she continued, "and I feel your presence there."

Isn't that the way we experience the presence of God?

5. *Expect That You Will Have Unrealistic Expectations of Him. Don't Expect to Progress at a Faster Maturation Level Than a Person Will Allow. Realize You Have a Need to Control and Master a Situation.*

The last few points can be easily considered together. They all involve you and what can be going on inside of you that can change a positive encounter into a negative one.

As you read the above three suggestions, I'm sure you can readily experience their meaning. I would, however, like to give you one humorous story as an illustration.

Several years ago I was working in an office that was furnished quite beautifully. There was sound equipment, tape recorders, and costly office equipment. Then there was a burglary which left the office vacant. I was furious! I had never experienced something like this before and I felt like I had been personally violated.

When the detective came to check on the case, I was horrified. He looked completely out of character in my estimation. His personal appearance was like something out of a horror movie, and I was disappointed. I had an unrealistic expectation of him.

Immediately I began my investigation of the detective. I insisted on knowing what was being done and further assumed that all our equipment would be recovered within the week. I expected faster progress than was realistically possible.

He was the expert. It was his job to search out and find a solution. Still, I wanted to control and master the situation.

These are ways we can cultivate fertile soil. Now let's consider how some people deplete their potentially rich soil.

6

FERTILE SOIL
VS.
SCRIPT

FERTILE SOIL VS. SCRIPT

The fertile soil of self-worth begins at birth and is enriched through a lifetime. The potency of these words and their meaning leads us to consider the alternative of fertile soil—script.

Eric Berne, in his last book "*What Do You Say After You Say Hello*," defines a script as "an ongoing program developed in early childhood under parental influence which directs individual behavior in most important aspects."

The healthy person (autonomous) does not live his life by a script. He is free to enjoy his own awareness, spontaneity and intimacy. We are, therefore, using the illustration of fertile soil synonymously with good health. The person who is unable to be free in his choices, behavior and relationships is living in and controlled by a script.

Scripts are commonly classified as tragic (harmartic) or banal. As the term obviously denotes, a tragic person living a tragic script is on a self-destructive course. The person living a banal script is not headed so much toward tragedy, but has acquiesced to "not winning." He's a non-winner. He has never maximized his life. So it is dull and non-fulfilling.

When in Tennessee, a gentleman came in to see me. Through his big smile it was easy to detect that he was burdened and attempting to reach out for help. Within 45 minutes he had related a tragic story that involved dropping out of school, drug abuse, several suicide attempts, wife beating and alcoholism. He was still young—only 32 years old. His physician's warning toward a potential fatal physical condition and his wife's threats of divorce brought him in to see me. He was living a tragic script. Later in this chapter, we will show how and why he made this decision.

At least once a week someone comes to our office with the following complaints:

1. I'm a loser.
2. I never do anything right.
3. I'm bored with everything.
4. Things are so-so in my life—nothing too exciting.
5. I've thought about changing, but it seems like too much trouble.
6. I'm 35 and I haven't done anything with my life yet.
7. I make a lot of plans but never follow through.
8. I have no intimacy in my life because it's too risky.
9. Our family has never been close.

10. I'm stuck in my situation. It's best that I don't cause waves.

These complaints come from men and women with non-winning scripts. Nothing terrible is happening but nothing good is happening either. In fact, nothing at all is happening.

A script decision is made in early childhood as a result of injunctions from parents and parent figures.

Claude Steiner states, "The injunction is always simply a prohibition, or an inhibition of the free behavior of the child. The injunction reflects the fears, wishes, anger and desires of the child in the parent."[10] In other words, when parents are under a great deal of stress, either because of the presence of the child or the behavior of the child, he or she will issue injunctions in order to cope.

Ten injunctions have been identified which bring about script decisions.[11] They are:

1. Don't be ...
2. Don't be you ...
3. Don't be your age ...
4. Don't succeed ...
5. Don't feel ...
6. Don't be close ...
7. Don't think ...

10. Claude Steiner, *Games Alcoholics Play* (New York: Ballantine) 1976, p. 35.
11. Robert Goulding, "New Decisions In T.A.: Creating An Environment For Redecision & Change" *In Progress In Group and Family Therapy*, editors Clifford Sager, M.D. and Helen Singer Kaplan, M.D., Ph.D., (New York: Brunner/Mazel Publishers) 1972.

8. Don't be well or sane . . .
9. Don't belong . . .
10. Don't . . .

Injunctions can be given both verbally and non-verbally. Obviously, survival is of utmost concern to children. In essence, this provides an effective means of control for parents and parental figures. "You will have my love, approval, support or protection if you don't . . ." Since the child needs strokes and protection from significant people in his life he will ultimately make the decision to "not be . . ." and the life script begins.

We want you to be familiar with these 10 major injunctions. At the same time, you should understand that the antithesis of an injunction is an allower. For every injunction, there is a healthy allower. The allowers make up the consistency of rich, fertile soil.

We will take a few injunctions and give a brief explanation or illustration along with its antithesis or allower.

I. *Don't Be*

We would like to refer you back again to our original example of a tragic script. The young man described himself as a high school dropout, a doper, a wife beater and an alcoholic with two attempted suicides. It really wouldn't take a psychologist to label his self-destructive behavior as a tragic script.

The remainder of his story points out the injunction and decision that began the script.

He was an unwanted child from the moment of

conception. As far back as he could remember there were negative comments about his birth. The abuse was not only verbal but also physical. His comments still come to our minds. "When I began to build things, draw pictures or color, I remember that nothing was ever stroked without some sort of a blemish. They always had to find something wrong with everything I did. I'm not sure when I made this decision, but I know I did. I decided that it simply was not worth it to live. After all, I wasn't supposed to have ever been born."

Antithesis: It's okay to be.

The warmth of you and the feeling of security tells the child she is wanted. Her birth and presence in the world and in the family is welcomed. It's a privilege to be her parents and to be able to offer her love, protection and support.

II. *Don't Be You.*

"A Man Named Sue" the song title goes, and thus a "don't be you" injunction.

Mother has a baby boy while Dad is away in the service. She had made her mind up that she wanted a girl. The son is never really accepted by the mother and she continually dresses him and conditions him to be feminine.

Antithesis: Be yourself.

The color of your skin, the shape of your body, your sex are all you. That's okay, and you are good!

III. *Don't Be a Child.*

Not too long ago we were eating dinner at a rather nice restaurant. It was quite crowded. While we were paying our check, a number of hungry people were waiting to be seated. Among those people were two well-meaning parents and their three children. The children were under four years of age. Yes, and they were tired, hungry and disturbed by the crowded room.

The mother and father became louder and louder in their commands. It was difficult not to look over our shoulders at the noisy scene.

"Sit down! Sit down!"

"You're disturbing people."

"What's the matter with you kids?"

"Shut your mouth and behave."

"Act like big people."

I nudged Dick and said, "Yes, and whatever you do, don't be a child!" There are other ways we can give this injunction. Ask yourself these questions:

1. Am I aware of the difficulties of childhood development?
2. Am I aware that children learn more from their feelings than their intellect?
3. Do I expect my younger child to sometimes respond as an adult?
4. Am I sensitive to my child's *need* to be a child?
5. Do my expectations of him exceed his maturation level or his ability to meet those expectations?
6. Do I dislike my child being a child?
7. Am I afraid that if my child acts like a child he will reflect on me as a parent?

8. Is my child acting like most other children her own age?
9. Is child behavior too inconvenient to me or stressful?
10. Do I feel it is more flattering to me as a parent to have a child who acts above his age?

IV. *Don't Grow Up.*

One of the great tragedies of life is a child who, because of neurological damage, does not mature mentally. Her body grows but her mental capacity is limited. This is sad, and is never easy to accept as a parent. However, some parents give the "Don't grow up" injunction to cope with various situations in life and to meet their own personal needs.

Mother may feel that she needs a little one around the house. Dad might continually refer to his daughter as "Daddy's baby" (even when she's a maturing young woman).

There's a lot of "don't think" and "don't succeed" also connected to keeping the child little. Over-protection as a parent is a successful tool of the "don't grow up" injunction.

We remember a young man who came to a weekend marathon that we conducted. We'll call him Bill although that was not his name. Bill was a handsome, athletic, 20-year-old man. He came to our weekend retreat to try and clarify some immediate issues in his life. The major problems always centered around his mother. By his own words he continually shouted his hate for his mom. She was in his way, causing problems and confusing issues according to his thinking. To add to his misery, he was terribly guilty. He was a Christian and had actively participated in the programs of the Church for years.

One of his questions to us and to the group went like this: "How can I grow up when my mom wants me to stay her little boy? And, how can I disappoint and disobey my mom and call myself a Christian?"

The group got into a heavy discussion which eventually resulted in a game of "Yes, but . . ."

Group: Why don't you explain your feelings to your mom?

Bill: I would, but she really believes she's right.

Group: You're of age. Don't ask. Tell her your plans.

Bill: I would, but I should honor her wishes as a Christian.

Group: If I were you, I'd lay it all out on the table and leave. You've got to make a break sometime.

Bill: I would, but she needs me!

We were getting nowhere so we moved to someone else who was more willing and ready to work on himself.

Later that evening, as we started group again, Bill wanted to begin first.

"I've made a decision," he proudly announced to the group. "I'm going to move out Monday whether she wants me to or not." As therapists, we were both fairly confident that there would be more to come, and that Bill's decision would take much more work than one simple decision. Nothing more was said that evening.

Toward the close of the marathon, Bill's body seemed tense and his behavior appeared out of character. We invited him to share his feelings.

This time Bill exploded with words of hate and disgust for himself and for his mother. "I can't leave her," he cried. "I need her as much as she needs me! I'm totally dependent upon her for everything."

Although Bill appeared to his friends and peers to be a normal, healthy, strong male, in reality he was a dependent child. The injunction had been given and reinforced. "Don't grow up!"

V. *Don't Think.*

This injunction was mentioned in our last example. In our experience, it is one of the most common injunctions. There are several reasons why this injunction is often given.

1. The need grownups have to do for their children.
2. False information as to what a good parent really is.
3. The unpleasant childhood of the parents (thus they want to over-protect their offspring).
4. The fear of a child who can indeed think.
5. The unwillingness to risk letting a child think for himself. (Being too much of a rescuer.)
6. Having to be in a "one up" position at all times.
7. Convinced that children can't think.

8. Playing, "What would they do without me," and "Look how hard I've tried," as a means of getting strokes.
9. Being too much into your own critical parent ego state and assuming your way is the right way.
10. The need to have the last word.

Some positive suggestions that say both verbally and non-verbally, "It's okay to think," would include:

1. Avoid rescuing the child from problem solving.
2. Give the child permission to think.
3. Give the child permission to fail.
4. Don't attempt to shield the child from the outside world—from life.
5. Develop your own life so you don't use the child to satisfy your own needs.
6. Avoid criticism when the child is trying to think.
7. Don't do it for him because you can do it better or faster.
8. Listen to your child without parental corrections to his statements.
9. Respect what he does and says. Respect him as a thinking person.

VI. *Don't Feel or Don't Show Your Feelings. Don't Be Close.*

Running a close second in our experiences to the "don't think" injunction are two others: (1) Don't feel, and (2) Don't be close.

We're keeping these two together in our explanation because they seem to go hand in hand.

Some comments that obviously suggest these injunctions are:

1. "Big boys don't cry."
2. "Girls don't show their anger."
3. "You don't hurt—stop crying."
4. "You don't hate your brother."
5. "Don't trust anyone."
6. "The world is out to get you."
7. "You can't depend on anyone."
8. "It's too dangerous to tell someone how you feel."
9. "Stay away from me and leave me alone."
10. "Don't touch me."

Even more potent than these statements are these silent cues to the child:

1. Insensitivity to the feelings of the child.
2. Harsh, inappropriate treatment of the child and others in the family.
3. An obvious lack of touching.
4. No sharing of intimacy.
5. A lack of caring within the family.
6. No one talking—really talking—in the family.
7. Mother or dad are never present.
8. Continually telling one another what the other does or does not feel.
9. Negatively stroking real feelings that cause stress to the parents or others.
10. Displaying fear or disapproval at the expression of real feelings.

When I was in my first year of high school, I wanted to become a member of an exclusive service club on campus. I knew that only three sophomores would be allowed to join. My chances were limited; yet I had my heart set on this social achievement. Sure, in retrospect, my motives were probably not the best and my logic poor. In my adolescent fervor, however, my confidence was high. The day came for the club to issue the invitations. One did not come to me. With equal adolescent intensity, I was crushed. My heart was broken, my pride gone and my ego shattered.

Upon sharing the bad news to those closest to me, these responses came:

My family said: "Go into your room until you stop crying. We don't want to hear it! Learn to be strong!"

My friends said: "You didn't want to be in the old club anyway."

My Christian friends said: "It must have been God's will, so don't feel bad."

If only someone would have said, "It must have hurt you terribly. I understand."

From that point on I attempted to dilute my feelings. I dared not express my feelings. I further doubted the purpose of a close relationship that rejected feelings.

VII. *Don't Succeed or Don't Be Important.*

Each of these could be individually defined. But

their meanings are so closely connected we will deal with them collectively.

The most commonly accepted life position is "I'm not okay. You are okay." That means that a host of people are living non-winners scripts. They are not being maximized and experience themselves in the victim position.

The Christian community is no exception. In fact, Christians can easily (but not truthfully) rationalize away the need to feel okay about being important and successful. The alibis come in packages marked:

"Humility"
"Too Proud To Be Good"
"This World Is Not My Home"
"Let Go and Let God"

Before you get upset and think I'm throwing out the truths in the above statements, read *further*! I am suggesting that we invalidate these truths when we exploit them to produce non-winners. If I give my child the "don't succeed" or "don't be important" injunctions, I am scripting him to be a loser or a non-winner. The exploitation of spiritual or Biblical concepts will be automatically used as an excuse to "cop-out" on productive, winning behavior. The child will grow up with a banal script. Even in his church life he will be confused, discouraged and depressed. The bad feeling payoff will be partly due to the double messages. In his Christian life he expects victory. He has a desire to really give something of himself to the Church. But he is fighting upstream because his script says, "don't succeed."

We have commented on the majority of injunctions. We would imagine by now that you are deep into thinking about you. That's good!

1. What injunctions have been passed on to you?
2. Which ones did you decide to accept?
3. What injunctions are you giving to your children?

The consequence of injunctions is scripting. Scripting acts as a deterrent to Christian growth. Injunctions are the rocks, weeds and insects hindering the growth of the Biblical seed in the individual and lead to a scripted life.

7

GAMES BIBLE

CHARACTERS PLAY

GAMES BIBLE CHARACTERS PLAY

We have both taught classes in churches, Bible schools and Christian organizations. In attempting to make application of the Scripture we have noticed an inability for some people to relate to the Bible characters as real people. Somehow people fantasize Peter, Paul, Martha or Moses as having no emotional needs, no physical desires and super human qualities. In doing so, we are limiting much of the Scripture's potency by suggesting:

1. "Martha was different. She knew Jesus in person."
2. "Paul was a super man. He could take it!"
3. "Moses was picked by God. No wonder he succeeded."

Bible characters were human beings just like you and me. They simply lived in a different day. There were advantages and certainly disadvantages compared to our day and age.

Psychological games are a reality. Being aware of them in your life will alert you as to when you're not being honest and intimate. To familiarize you with the concept of games, the way they are played and the possible consequences, we have chosen to reflect on the games Bible characters played.

First, let's review the idea of games. Eric Berne introduced the idea of psychological games in his book *Games People Play*. In his last book *What Do You Say After You Say Hello?* he defined games as sets of ulterior transactions, repetitive in nature with a well-defined psychological payoff."[12]

To make it very simple, the ulterior transaction is the transaction that appears to be one thing but is really another. This is called a con. Repetitive in nature means that we usually play the same games in the same way, using the same words with the same people. We have specific games that reinforce our life's position. For example, a person in the "I'm not okay, you're okay" position experiences himself as a victim and continually sets himself up in the "Kick Me" game to prove it.

A well defined psychological payoff means that dishonesty in the form of a psychological game always leads to a payoff. The payoff consists of bad feelings.

There are a number of reasons why people play games. For further study, we would suggest you read the books listed in the bibliography. For the present, however, we want to point out that the two

---

12. Eric Berne, *What Do You Say After You Say Hello*. (New York: Grove Press, Inc.) 1972.

major reasons for games are: (1) to get strokes, (2) to reinforce the life's position (I'm not okay, you are okay).

Let your magic carpet whirl you back all the way to the days of Adam. Let's catch him and others in their games, and in doing so, learn something about ourselves.

Moses

The children of Israel had been in bondage for hundreds of years. Their wills were weakening. The ravished bodies of the men weakened under the whip of Pharoah's soldiers, the bellies of the children swelled from hunger and the women cried for peace again in Israel.

In the midst of their groanings, God heard their request and chose a leader who was destined to be their deliverer.

> When the Lord saw that he turned aside to look. God called to him from the midst of the bush, and said, "Moses, Moses!" And he said, "Here I am."
>
> "And now, behold, the cry of the sons of Israel has come to Me; furthermore, I have seen the oppression with which the Egyptians are oppressing them. Therefore, come now, and I will send you to Pharoah, so that you may bring My people, the sons of Israel, out of Egypt."
>
> But Moses said to God, "Who am I, that I should go to Pharoah?"

God had announced His confidence in Moses and assured him of His support and backing. Moses immediately began to play one of the most obvious "Yes, but" games ever recorded in history. The Lord continued to give Moses adult information. God would give a reasonable explanation and Moses would respond with a "Yes, but I'm not . . ." (it all added up to not being worthy).

In desperation, Moses then switched to the game of "Stupid." "Please Lord, I have never been eloquent . . . for I am slow of speech and slow of tongue."

God refused to let Moses discount himself and the wisdom of his Lord. Instead, he changed his transactions with Moses (became parental) and gave Moses direct messages, adult information, and nurturing support. The games were over, and Moses began his mission of deliverance.

Cain and Abel

There was a disturbance in the first family. In Genesis 4:3 we see Cain initiate the game of "Uproar" by bringing an incorrect offering to the Lord. He knew that his gift would be unacceptable. Cain discounted God's request and also the offering of his brother, Abel. Uproar is a game where conflict is purposefully started to avoid intimacy. When God did not join him in his game, but rather gave adult information such as: "If you do well, will not your countenance be lifted up?" Cain played a third degree game of "Uproar" and killed his brother, Abel.

Cain was also playing a game of "Stupid." He knew quite well the correct offering to bring to the Lord. Further, when God (knowing that Cain had killed his brother) asked, "Where is your brother? Where is Abel?" Cain retorted, "How should I know? Am I supposed to keep track of him wherever he goes?" This is obviously a game of "Stupid."

Upon hearing his punishment, Cain replied, "My punishment is greater than I can bear." Cain was into the "Ain't it awful?" game.

A review will focus in on the emotional state of the one initiating the game—Cain.

1. Uproar: A game played from the "Blameless" position. The player involved refuses to accept responsibility with or without an effort for forgiveness.

2. Stupid: Stupid is played from the "I'm not okay. You're okay" position with an invitation to "kick me."

3. Ain't it awful (Hang Dog) is also played from a "not-okay position" and in Cain's situation, destruction was in its payoff.

Jonah

Who hasn't heard of Jonah? At least the big fish is well known to all.

The story is exciting, but the critics deny its validity. I do not find it difficult to believe the literal account of the story. Jesus validates its significance when He states in Matthew 12:40:

"For as Jonah was in the great fish for three days and three nights, so I, the Messiah, shall be in the heart of the earth three days and three nights" (The Living Bible).

Jonah was no exception when it came to playing games. God told Jonah to go to the great city of Ninevah.

"But Jonah was afraid to go and ran away from the Lord" (Jonah 1:3, The Living Bible).

Jonah was into a second degree game of "Cops and Robbers." According to Eric Berne in *Games People Play*, the thesis of this game is "See if you can catch me."[13] It's similar to the game we all played in childhood called hide-and-seek.

In his not-okay position he tried to run from God by boarding a ship leaving for Tarshish.

The story's adventure continues to unfold. Somehow as I read it once again the humor emerges more than before. A grown man makes himself a fugitive in his own mind, sinks into fear and despair, and crawls into a dark corner of a ship to hide from the Lord.

Not only is that a game of "Cops and Robbers," it's absurd!

Jonah was playing "Kick Me," of course, and when a threatening storm arose he immediately said, "Throw me out into the sea . . . and it will become calm again . . . for I know this terrible storm has come because of me."

Paul

Who do you admire most in Scripture? There are many admirable Biblical characters. Frankly, David is the man with whom I most identify. He seemed to run the gamut of human experience. In some cases, he praised God in the highest terms. At other times he pleaded for protection from his enemies much like a frightened child. Sometimes, he even tried to manipulate God by reminding Him of His promises. We can easily see the different games that David played with God. But what about Paul, the Apostle? Paul was a fiery, dedicated person who seemed to be as zealous in perpetuating the Kingdom of God as anyone we have read about in Scripture. What games did Paul play?

Some of you may say, "He didn't play any games." Now wait a minute. Paul was inspired but he was not divine. Sometimes we attribute a quality to the saints of Scripture that may not be true.

Let's see if Paul didn't play some games. In 2 Corinthians 11, Paul states the trials he went through such as imprisonment, beatings and humiliation. Perhaps Paul was playing "Pity Me."

At another point Paul boasts of servicing the community of believers for no pay. This could be the game called, "See what I've done for you."

In other portions of Scripture, Paul tells believers that he has worked hard and long in their behalf.

Without him they would still be in their wretched conditions. This may be a game called, "What would you do without me?"

Adam and Eve

The terrifying feeling struck at his heart like sudden thunder. His body seemed to reel, his legs fought hard to support him, his brain burned with fear and disbelief. It was a new feeling, one he had never experienced before. He found himself crying out like a man drowning in a stormy sea.

> "The woman whom Thou gavest to be with me, she gave me from the tree and I ate."

You recall the situation. Both Eve and Adam ate of the forbidden fruit. God approached them, asked what had happened and Adam responded by blaming Eve, and Eve blamed the serpent.

Is this a game? Of course it is. The game is "If it weren't for you." Adam was blaming God because if Eve had not been created for him there would have been no temptation to eat of the apple. Was it God's fault? Apparently Adam in his fear felt that it was.

How many times have you done the same thing? I don't believe I have ever had an accident of any sort that my first reaction wasn't to blame the other person or object. One time I accidentally ran into a door. I recall my first reaction, "What's that door doing there, anyway?"

David and Uriah

Read 2 Samuel 11:15. Do you recall the story? David fell in love with Uriah's wife. The king had great power in those days and if he wanted something he usually got it. Of course, we all know the abuse of power can corrupt the soul of the person in power. David wanted the woman so he ordered Uriah to fight in a battle where he was sure to be killed. The payoff for the game was the woman, but what a price David paid.

The game in T.A. is called "Now I've got you, you S.O.B." This game is played where we have something on the other person. We have a control over them and we misuse that power to gain something for ourselves.

In speaking to a class one night a woman flatly declared she would never use that game. She said her husband often comes home late which makes her angry. Later she slipped and said, "Just wait until our next argument, I'll sure remind him of it." A clear intention to play, "Now I've got you, you S.O.B."

Peter

But Peter said, "Man, I don't know what you are talking about" (Luke 22:60).

Peter, the burly fisherman, tanned by years in the sun, firm in his declaration of love for Christ, played "Stupid." Why? He had walked with the Master, heard Him speak and ate of the same food. How could he deny knowing the Christ? Had he not

109

seen Jesus cause the lame to walk, the blind to see, the dead to rise? Seems absurd doesn't it? Yet, Peter played "Stupid" when asked if he knew Jesus.

What was the payoff for Peter? Well, I would imagine Peter was afraid. Have you ever been in a position where everything you believed in was in doubt? The fisherman had witnessed the authority of Jesus, now he saw his Lord bound and led by angry men to be judged by lesser men. How could this be? Now Peter's own safety was in question. The payoff was to protect himself from harm and danger.

For years I have attended meetings in my profession where the question of basic religious beliefs has been one of the subjects of conversation. Almost everyone there, in one way or another, lets it be known that to believe in a "fable" that happened so many years ago is less than intelligent. Perhaps the question may be addressed to me, "What do you believe?"

I have to say, one of my first impulses is to play "Stupid" and answer with an obvious put-off—I just don't know. I have never done it for I know that temporary benefits may feel O.K. but tomorrow's dawning will bring shame and loss of self-esteem.

Joseph

"The Hebrew slave you've had around here tried to rape me, and I was only saved by my screams. He fled, leaving his jacket behind" (Genesis 39:17, 18, The Living Bible).

Joseph was in Egypt, a slave, in the house of Potiphar. The wife of Potiphar was sexually attracted to the handsome Hebrew and tried to seduce him. The seductive game in T.A. is called "Rapo."

When Joseph refused her, she set about to trap and punish him. Of course, she told her husband and he was angry.

> Well, when her husband heard his wife's story, he was furious. He threw Joseph into prison where the king's prisoners were kept in chains (Genesis 39:19, The Living Bible).

The wife was playing, "Let's you and him fight."

The two games—"Rapo" and "Let's you and him fight"—illustrate a specific ego position on the part of the wife. She was in the position of "I'm okay, you're not okay." In the game, "Rapo," she attempted to put Joseph in the victim position. When he refused to respond to her advances she switched the game and persecuted him.

Joseph remained in his ego position of "I'm okay, you're okay" because he continued to respect his own sense of integrity and that of the employer. Actually, Joseph was never in the victim's position because he refused to play the game. Of course, Joseph suffered physically by being thrown into prison but even there he still retained his okay position.

Judas

Judas, too, had asked Him, "Rabbi, am I
the one?" And Jesus had told him, "Yes."

Matthew 26:25

Did you ever wonder why Judas asked Jesus that
question? Was it that Judas wondered if his plot had
been discovered? I would seriously doubt that Judas
believed in the divinity of Christ. I suspect that
Judas saw Christ as a man with authority who could
be used to further a movement of which Judas was a
part. The intent of Judas was to "use" Jesus to
accomplish his own aims. When people play games
such as these it is called, "Let's pull a fast one on
Joey."

The ego position is "I'm not okay, you're not
okay." In this game a switch takes place between
the victim and the aggressor. The payoff is to use the
other person (victim), but quite often the game is
reversed and the aggressor becomes the victim.
Judas is a prime example of this game.

Some psychological games have been mentioned
in this chapter. There are many more examples of
games that Bible characters played. The list of
games played from different ego states, positions
and transactions would require a book.

Has this helped you to understand the basic
characters and personalities of the men and women
in Scripture? We hope so. Remember the individuals of Scripture are just like you and me. Some
were faced with greater problems, experienced

more temptations and sometimes failed more than you.

We all face daily the kinds of choices they had to make. We can learn from their mistakes and successes.

Perhaps we have created a renewed interest in your reading of the Scripture. It is our hope that the people of the Scripture rise to meet you in a vital living way. Let them talk to you. Experience and share with them their heartaches and joys. Listen and you will hear their secrets.

8

GAMES
CHRISTIANS PLAY

GAMES CHRISTIANS PLAY

"I think we should really pray about Susie and John. They are having problems and they might get a divorce."

Everyone had been quiet—now they were *really* quiet. People looked at each other. Looks of disbelief and amazement fell across some faces. The congregation became especially quiet but people stirred restlessly.

The setting—a midweek prayer service. The opening hymns had been sung, announcements were made and now the pastor had called for prayer requests. The usual requests were mentioned.

Some people had noticed John and Susie were not present. Their absence was obvious because they were always there. In fact, Frank said, "Wonder where John is? Probably home watching the game." Frank smiled as he dismissed his own question.

Then a dear saint rose and made her request. "I think we should pray for Susie and John."

Sounds like a normal, caring and interested

statement, doesn't it? Perhaps it is, but maybe it isn't so innocent. Maybe a game is being played.

Let's say, for example, that John and Susie were not having problems. Or let's say they did not want everyone in the church to know about it even if they were going through a problem time. Whatever assumption we might make, at this point everyone in the church "knew" Susie and John were having problems.

You recall from Chapter Two what a game is. Let's have a short review. A psychological game is played to get strokes. Essentially, a game has a gimmick of some sort. Usually, a game involves an ulterior transaction.

In the case of our dear saint, she was revealing private information in order to let everyone know she had special knowledge about people in the church. Her position in the congregation was greatly enhanced and her personal sense of strength and power elevated.

The dear sister got her strokes, but possibly John and Susie, and maybe others, suffered from private knowledge being made public.

An ulterior transaction always has a hidden meaning. Quite often we are not aware of those two meanings, but we can still be destructive to others and actually ourselves when we play games.

There are many forms of ulterior transactions, some are subtle, others more obvious. Do you recall the one for Zest soap—"For once in your life be really clean." The implication is that unless I use

Zest soap I am doomed to always be dirty. Or it may imply I have never been clean in my life.

I can almost hear some of you say, "Christians wouldn't do that, they wouldn't play games like that." Christians not only would but they do play games like that. This may sound like a harsh statement but it is based on observation.

In our experiences we have found that Christians are basically concerned with being okay people. When they are not acting as okay people we feel it is because they are largely unaware of their hidden motives and feelings. Our intention is to assist in the discovery of hidden motives and feelings which will contribute to a richer life. We believe that Christian people are generally sincere in finding answers to the everyday task of living the abundant life.

The discovery of the games we play will help immensely in helping us to feel good about ourselves and others.

The example we gave at the beginning of the chapter is a game we call, "Let's pray while we gossip."

Keep in mind that every time you hear such a request it may not be a game. However, be aware that people play games without always being conscious of them.

Another rather common game is called, "Hi Ho Hawkeye."

Sharon is a delightful person. She has many talents. She sings in the choir, bakes a mean cake, and is truly a helping person. Besides being very pretty, she is witty and intelligent. There is not a single meeting in the church that Sharon does not attend. A real asset to the church. She is a very determined young woman who feels her mission field is her church. She watches over the congregation with great concern.

I know Sharon quite well because I have been asked to speak at her church a number of times. My first meeting with her was rather interesting. Upon hearing that I was a psychologist she felt that she had better listen to what I had to say very carefully. Psychologists can be tricky, you know. Naturally, she came up to see me after I finished speaking. She said she enjoyed it but, "remember, Doctor, you see most everything from a psychological point of view, not a spiritual one."

After several visits to the church, I again had the opportunity of her evaluation of me. She stated, "You know, Doctor, you have matured a lot spiritually."

What was she really saying to me? As I was able to know Sharon better I accepted that she needed to hear statements which met her approval. I also learned that she was overly concerned with everyone else's "spiritual condition," including the pastor. She was the self-appointed watchdog of the church.

Much of the messages that Sharon gives to people is, "I'm okay, you're not okay and I had better tell you when you're not okay." What's wrong with this attitude? Well, the Christian life should be one of sharing. "Share each other's troubles and problems, and so obey our Lord's command" (Galatians 6:2, The Living Bible).

In T.A. the game is called, "I'm only trying to help you." The life position is that of the rescuer, but the results are to make the other person feel angry, guilty and hurt.

The payoff that Sharon receives from her game-playing is to be slightly superior, which ultimately avoids intimacy. After all, who can relate to such a parent figure when you are under a microscope and every statement is evaluated? Probably, Sharon is admired but not very well liked.

Another game people often play in church is "What's wrong with the way it is?"

Recently many people had been complaining that they would like to sing some of the newer hymns or songs that had been written. The complaints got back to the pastor and he brought it up at the next meeting of the music committee. George seemed annoyed but was silent. The pastor, a sensitive person, inquired as to George's withdrawal from the conversation. A slight but well controlled trace of anger crept into George's retort when he stated, "We have to be careful, often the decline of any church begins subtly with these kind of changes. After all, music appeals to the emotions, we know the songs we use really bring out the Gospel. Besides, what's wrong with the songs we sing? We've been singing them for years."

George was right. They had been singing them

for years and the lack of interest from the congregation showed it.

George was playing a game. Actually, George is afraid of growth. He likes his security. Anything that threatens him makes him fearful.

A game such as, "What's wrong with the way it is?" is similar to a game in T.A. called "It's too soon to terminate."

George is actually in an ego position of "I'm not okay, you're okay." His fears are that the church family will ask him to give up that feeling of security which comes with staying with old and tried behavior.

The payoff for George is to remain the same perpetual child who takes no risks.

Growing up can be fearful. Probably most of you know that. A church is like a person, it goes through stages of development. Sometimes it begins as an excited child spreading its enthusiasm like ripe oranges dropping from a lush, fruit-bearing tree. But it must continue to grow.

The church must be able to say, "When I was a child, I used to speak as a child, think as a child, reason as a child; when I became a man, I did away with childish things" (I Corinthians 13:11, NAS).

The "Hollow Halo" game is similar to the one in T.A. called "Ain't it awful?"

An example would be where Joe counsels others on the pitfalls of not praying enough. Can you hear some of his admonitions? "Prayer changes things. Pray without ceasing," or, "I take every opportunity to talk with God that's available to me." Joe really believes what he says and so do we. Everyone in church knows Joe's stock answer to all problems—"Pray about it."

Does Joe's life reflect his counsel? Maybe it doesn't. Joe is constantly involved in one bad choice after another. Recently he changed jobs, giving up a secure but average income position because Joe had prayed about it and "God led me to take this new job, make extra money and then tithe it to the Lord's work." Just last month Joe lost his new job and is now drawing unemployment. Joe isn't seriously looking for a new job, but he's praying about it.

I'll bet if you talked to Joe about any problem, he would tell you to pray about it.

What we are saying here is the "Hollow Halo" game is played where the person easily sees your mistakes, offers advice as to your "bad situation," tells you what to do. However, the person does not cope with the failure, mistakes and errors of his own life. He is spending his time in dealing with the "sins" of others and neglecting his own internal household.

The ego position that Joe is taking is "I'm O.K., you're not O.K." He attempts to rescue the world while "losing his own soul." The payoff for Joe is to establish his "parent role."

We have described some games, told you about the ego positions and mentioned the payoff. We are sure you could list games you have observed in your

Christian life. We would like to list some more games. See if they fit. Again, be open and try to apply them to yourself. Don't be afraid or defensive. Or if you are defensive you can rest assured we are "meddling" in your life.

Read this list of some other games and see if they apply to you and your church experiences.

"You can do more...more...more..." is a game where a person is made to feel like a victim. No matter what you do it is not enough. Somehow you are made to feel guilty even though to the best of your ability you are doing all that you can.

The game involves a persecutor and victim. The victim accepts that he can do more, but in reality he can't. He ends up feeling like a failure.

The answer appears to be getting into your adult ego state and structuring your time realistically in order to evaluate the effort and time that you can devote to any project.

The following questions may help you avoid playing the victim game.

1. List your priorities—family, job, church, activities involved in each of these.
2. Evaluate yourself—do you play the victim role in various patterns of your total life.
3. Honestly estimate what you are doing. Perhaps you are doing too much already and not performing at a satisfactory level.
4. Ask yourself—can I say no? If you can't you are playing this game from a victim position.
5. Ask yourself—what does responsibility mean?

Can I share it with others or do I need to do everything myself.

"Sorry you weren't here" is played from a persecutor's position. You tell someone you are sorry they were not at prayer meeting last week. The underlying messages maybe—how come you are rejecting your responsibilities.

The typical rescuer plays the "What if I weren't here" game. He feels the church would cease to exist if he were not present to insure its safety. After all, nobody can speak, teach, play the organ or run business meetings like he can. The payoff is the only way he can feel important is by his activities not because he is himself. The ego position is "I'm not O.K."

The "heads I win, tails you lose" game says "My sin is O.K., but yours aren't." It's O.K. for me to gossip but don't you dare smoke. Or, it's O.K. for me to "constructively" criticize the pastor, but don't you dare tell me I'm wrong in my interpretation of scripture.

"Piety in Poverty" is an important game. Often a person may placate his non-success by priding himself on his lack of accomplishment. Such as, I have successfully stayed poor in order to serve God better. Pride is often the ulterior transaction in a piety oriented statement. Frankly, we see nothing wrong in seeing a bumper sticker on a Mercedes which reads "Jesus Saves." God does not require poverty of you—only faith.

"I Love You, if . . ." is a common game. For

example, George is a great guy. You really see things alike. George is easy to love because his views do not disagree with yours. Sometimes love becomes very conditional. This type of love is based on agreement, not allowing the other person to be himself.

Real love tolerates, allows and accepts the individual differences between people. In fact, real love maximizes the other person and assists the other person in creating his own values, ideals and self-actualized personality. To make agreement a condition of love is to attempt to manipulate the other person into being another you.

Love should be free from manipulation.

"What's there to cry about now?" is a subtle game. A person may pursue a certain goal for a long time. The goal is stated repeatedly without being met. Then suddenly the goal is realized, where does the person go next. Suppose a parent continually asks for support from the church group because of a wayward child. The group gives the asked for strokes. Then the child's bad behavior is corrected. What will the person do next to get strokes from the group.

"Yes, but" . . . is a game in T.A. similar to "I couldn't quite make it." In "I couldn't quite make it," the person takes the victim position always explaining his various failures at jobs, home, church, etc. If he is given constructive alternatives, he discounts them by telling everyone, "Well, I tried that but it didn't work because I didn't have what it takes."

As a consequence everyone is always boosting his morale and trying to help. The person gets his strokes from so much attention but is reinforced in his feelings of inadequacy.

Of all the games, "Let God do it" may be the most often played.

I am reminded of a woman who came to our office a number of years ago. She had serious problems in her relationships. She felt separate from her husband, distant from her children, and rejected by others. Mrs. X had a good job, was always in church and actively pursued prayer and Bible reading. Her problems centered around her relationships with people. I asked her, "What are you doing about your problems?" She replied "Oh, I pray every morning about them. Let me insert here, she had no difficulty in talking. She talked continually about her problems. So I knew she could talk. I suggested she stop praying about her problems. She looked at me in amazement and suspicion. I assume she wanted me to show her a new way to pray. Instead I suggested she talk to others about anything but her problems, no matter what, and do something herself.

You probably have guessed by now what she was doing. She wanted God to do what He had already done—give her the ability to relate, share and interact with others.

What she needed to work on was how to be a

friendly person. You can only do that by practicing being friendly. She worked with me for a period of time, taking the responsibility for her own self, and today she gives God the credit.

There is a fine line between our responsibilities to do something ourselves and then letting God work where only *He* can work.

These are just a few of the games Christians play. Remember a game defines a behavior. Since there are many forms of behavior which rob us of the fulfilled life, games can be played and defined endlessly. Our concern is that we stop playing games.

A game is played to get strokes. We must ask ourselves are the strokes worth it. If I play "pity me" and constantly tell you about my misfortunes, how long will it take before you will want to avoid me.

Your question might be "Well, I realize that I am playing games, but how do I stop?" Let us suggest some ways of not playing games.

1. Realize that you do play games.
2. Be aware of the kind of games you play.
3. Avoid the triangle of victim, persecutor, rescuer.
   A. Do not allow yourself to be victimized.
   B. Let people do things for themselves, don't always rescue them.
   C. Do not try to seek power or mastery by persecuting others.
4. Be aware that a game involves a discount. By

that we mean you or someone else is going to be put down. A potential or existing relationship will be injured.

5. Look at your behavior, find the behavior that produces the greatest fear, anger and hate, and realize that games center around these feelings.
6. Make choices—games are usually repeated behaviors which have temporary benefits but long term destructive results.
7. Do some risking—be honest and open. Start gradually, one step at a time. It may be fearful but it's worth the effort.
8. Examine your motives. The dear saint who told about John and Susie, may have wanted attention for herself. There are better ways of getting attention.
9. Learn to ask for your strokes. If your husband does not comment on your carefully prepared dinner, ask him how he liked it.
10. Accept your needs and know them. Sometimes we are masters at denying our needs. "I don't need anyone." That's absurd. You do need close intimate relationships.

Underlying all of life is a need for closeness and intimacy. We recently heard of some studies where various animals risked their lives for the safety of their mates. Your pet lives for your strokes. Creation strives to be heard, loved and recognized. These are not sentimental words, but reality. Survival is not the driving force of nature. Loving and being loved is. God created that reality, we merely react to it.

Games actually subvert the plans of God. To be in a right relationship with God, we must become what we have described as a person who is aware, spontaneous and intimate. This means autonomy. Autonomy is the ability to depend because we make the choice to depend. We cannot play games with God. He knows it all. We can make an autonomous choice to depend on him and be independent of the needs for games.

9

EGO STATES OF JESUS

EGO STATES OF JESUS

*"For as you know him better, he will give
you, through his great power, everything
you need for living a truly good life."*
II Peter 1:3, The Living Bible

Who doesn't want to live a "truly good life?" I do.
I'm sure you do too. What does this kind of life
really mean? What sources do we turn to for help.

For years I have heard "become more like
Christ," "practice living like Jesus," or "live the
Christ-like life." These are all true and valid
statements. But the trick is—how do I live a
Christ-like life?

Well, let's consider an obvious answer. Do what
Jesus did. Following his example.

This could only be a partial solution. For instance,
if we tried to follow the example of a famous writer
like E. Stanley Jones in our work, we would sound
strange. Only E. Stanley Jones can write like E.
Stanley Jones.

Secondly, it's possible to follow only the behavior

of Christ and not experience the same feelings Jesus had when he was performing that behavior.

Remember, we are to "have the mind of Christ." Just doing what Jesus did unaccompanied by the reasons and feelings Jesus experienced may make us poor imitators.

Someone once said "I cannot tell you about Freudian Psychology, I can only give you my interpretation of Freudian Psychology."

We want to learn to think, feel and know as Jesus did. We want his mind to be in us. We want our choices and decisions to be made from the standpoint that Jesus is within us. We want to be "perfected unto all good works, because we are like him."

Let us suggest a way that may help us to know him better and better. This would be to know his ego states when he was transacting in a variety of situations.

Let's review briefly the various ego states.

Child Ego State: This is the state that contains our feelings, drives and motivations. Of course, there are various parts to it.

There is the charming kid which is fun-loving, seeks pleasure, finds beauty. The tender caring feelings of love come from this position.

There is also the uncharming part which is rebellious, manipulative and seeks its own way.

Key words that describe this state are, "I want..."

Parent Ego State: This state contains the values,

ideals and morals that we have and take from the "Big People" in our life.

The parent ego state has a critical part and a nurturing part.

Key words are; should, have to go, got to, etc.

Adult Ego State: This is the logical and rotund part of us that is something like a computer.

The main characteristics of the adult ego state are:

1. Information gathering
2. Logical
3. Non-emotional
4. Reality testing

What we would like to do is to take some examples from scripture involving the life of Jesus and determine which ego state Jesus was in while transacting with that situation.

It should be noted that a well handled transaction depends on the appropriate ego state applied properly to the situation.

An example would be when Jesus wept over Jerusalem. He was apparently in his tender caring child ego state. His behavior was appropriate to the situation because he saw tragedy inherent to that city and its people.

Let's pause for just a moment to note that when we use the term child ego state we are not referring to childish behavior.

Quite often we find that men confuse childish behavior with allowing feelings to come from their Child Ego State. Jesus' crying meant that He was free to cry. Many men in our society are scripted to believe that crying is either childish or feminine. We wonder how many other feelings are buried beneath misconceptions and faulty information.

To express our Child Ego State as Jesus did is a sign of the truly autonomous person.

In Matthew 15:32 we read about Jesus feeding 5,000 people.

"I feel compassion for the multitude," He said.

The application here is that Jesus had tremendous feelings for the welfare and hunger needs of people. You remember the story, he fed them.

Having this kind of compassion for the multitudes comes from the nurturing part of our Parent Ego State.

His caring in this incident involved meeting the physical needs of the people. The people were hungry and that was a reality of life.

In our Christian ministry we are sometimes more effective in our witness as we minister to another's physical needs.

As I write this, I'm thinking of an evening several months ago. It was a meeting involving several people who wanted to discuss their spiritual and psychological condition. I particularly recall a young woman who sat on the floor rather disheveled in appearance, chattering rather aimlessly. Seemingly she wanted to be part of the group and participate in the conversation. I remember thinking of her as being disorganized and confused as she groped for words which would connect with her feelings and experience of other people. I thought, "that poor young woman is on the verge of some emotional breakdown." A distinct feeling came that I wanted to soothe her as I would a small child and tell her all would be okay. At that point she was unresponsive to any hand that might be extended to her. But that distinct feeling I had was compassion, and I was a part of my nurturing parent state.

We have found that sensitivity to another person is one of the main attributes of nurturing. Let us extend the concept of sensitivity to the nature of love itself. Can love really exist unless one person is sensitive to the needs of another and attempts to maximize that person?

Imagine yourself in the crowd witnessing this encounter between Jesus and the Pharisees. Would you have been protective of Jesus, or would you have stood in wonder as to how He would get out of this predicament.

It was common knowledge that the Pharisees were out to trap Him.

"Tell us therefore, what do you think?
Is it lawful to give a poll tax to
Caesar or not?"

With this question, they initiated a game of "corner." This is a perfect example of a duplex transaction. (Two transactions at the same time.) On the social level they were asking a simple question. On the psychological (hidden) level, they were saying, "We've got you cornered."

Jesus was aware of their ego state.

"But Jesus perceived their malice . . ."

Collectively, the Pharisees were in their critical Parent Ego State. They approached Jesus, however, from their "Little Professor." The Little Professor is the adult within the child ego. It is the part of the child that is clever, sly and even manipulative.

From His controlling parent, He commanded them to bring Him the coin. This moved Him into a position of authority. He then gave them adult information.

"Render unto Caesar what is Caesar's,
and to God what is God's."

The game ended. Jesus had given the perfect response. Rather than having been cornered, the Scriptures say: "And hearing this they marvelled, leaving Him, they went away."

There's a lesson for all of us in this example. When we experience that a person is in her critical parent, and is wanting to trip us up, adult information will often curb the problem.

All my life I've heard the saying, "You don't discuss religion or politics." Of course, this isn't so, but the reason behind this archaic notion is the intensity of feeling connected with both. There's nothing as severe as a Holy War.

Usually when a person has a critical parent notion about you and your faith it may proceed into a game of "Corner NIGY" or "Uproar." Be careful not to "bite." Do as Jesus did in His transaction.

When I attended the University of Tennessee, I made many beautiful friends who were studying for their teaching credential. Most of them, however, were not into the Christian faith. Some of them who had been reared in the Church were rebelling and spoke out harshly against the religious community.

I was having coffee one morning before class with some of my fellow students. A young man whom I had not previously met sat down beside me. He began critically but cleverly to antagonize me. The conversation went something like this:

Student: You're one of those religious nuts aren't you?

Me: I'm not familiar with that term.

Student: Well, you go around reading the Bible.

Me: I find it an excellent piece of literature.

Student: I'm an evolutionist.

Me: I find that theory very interesting.

Student: Come on now, you know what I mean. You believe in all that God stuff?

Me: My faith is quite adequate for me.

It worked, he actually threw up his arms, chuckled and said to the others, "It's no use, I can't win."

"Jesus made a whip from some ropes and chased them all out and drove out the sheep and oxen, scattering the money changers' coins over the floor and turning over their tables!"

"Enough is enough! You've gone too far. This behavior has got to stop!" These words have been uttered millions of times by parents throughout the ages. Any parental figure (teacher, parent, principal, employer, governmental official) must be willing to step in and take action when necessity calls. The laws of our land do just that. The Supreme Court is the last word on legal matters. Jointly, its Judges say, "Enough! This is the law!"

Occasionally, a misunderstanding exists that has no need for the controlling Parent Ego State. Usually this is a misunderstanding.

I've been in situations more times than I like to remember when I literally saved a life by bringing energy to my parent and taking control.

"Jesus got mad! He lost his head there for a moment," the critic reminded me. "On the contrary," I replied, "He shaped things up." You've got to really stretch a point to condemn this as inappropriate behavior. Had Jesus not taken complete control, things would have continued and no doubt become worse.

It was a festive occasion. The comparison could be made to today's carnival spirit. Everyone was there. People, animals and especially business were present. Even the religious leaders were exploiting the people. The noise alone must have made the situation unbearable.

A slight suggestion from a mild appearing teacher would have never gotten results. It would take an episode of power to even get anyone's attention. So, in his controlling parent, Jesus broke up a sad, disgusting scene and turned it into a forecast of His death and resurrection.

"What right do you have to order them out?"
the Jewish leaders demanded.

They question Jesus, but He has already taken authority, acted with authority and achieved His goal.

"If you have the authority from God, show us
a miracle."
"All right," Jesus replied, "this is the
miracle I will do for you: Destroy this
sanctuary and in three days I will raise
it up!"

Many people left the celebration (the Scriptures continue to tell us) believing because of His miracles.

Several years ago, I was at a church retreat in Palm Springs. It was a warm, balmy afternoon near sundown. I had just cut open a ripe, juicy watermelon when a disturbance near the pool caught my attention.

I ran to see the problem only to find the pastor lying flat on his back at the edge of the pool. A careless youth had pushed him, and he had lost his balance and fallen. The moment I saw him I knew he was in terrible pain.

The people surrounding him were becoming hysterical. I had to collect my controlling parent or these people were going to devastate this man's chances for relief and medical attention. Only after I cleared the crowd away, could I nurture the injured pastor. Oh yes, I was later criticized for my "non-caring attitude" when I refused to be hysterical and chose to be helpful.

But the results are all that matters.

With Jesus, a wrong was made right in the temple, and adult conversion proceeded with his critics and many believed.

In my example, the pastor was allowed privacy and quiet, an ambulance called and a potential disaster turned out okay.

> *"And it happened that as He was reclining at the table in the house, behold many tax gatherers and sinners came and joined Jesus and His Disciples."*
>
> *"[at Matthew's house there were many notorious swindlers there as Guests.]"*

The scene is easy to picture, isn't it. Jesus saw the worth of a man named Matthew and wanted to become his friend and maximize him as a person.

He accepted Matthew where he was, and in a non-judging position he attended a dinner party at his house. It was easily apparent to the on-lookers and curiosity seekers that the guest list was not like the typical church membership list.

This story, as well as the Marriage Feast at Canaan reveals the Child Ego State of Jesus. Remember again, we do not mean childishness or immaturity. The natural child is part of us that lets us enjoy life and one another. Jesus relaxed and in His child He shared enjoyable social moments with Matthew and his friends. These friends, remember, were not normally in His immediate social circle. In fact, the Scriptural account is explicit in pointing out that they were the scoundrels or misfits of the community.

Because of His divine compassion, He showed human spontaneity and this resulted in an evening of relating with men who would have never heard His truths. The divine characteristics of love and goodness were manifest through the warmth and charisma of His human side.

Throughout the years this illustration has shaken the very foundation of the sterile and pompous church. The laughter of Jesus haunts those whose piety shields them from the burdens of others. Jesus, by His own example, tore down the thrones of the clergy and offered them a chair, a bench or a picnic table in the midst of humanity.

"Why does your teacher associate with men like that?"

That was the question of the religious community. To the Pharisees and to all others who would hesitate to live and love and relate to all classes of people, Jesus replied:

"Because people who are well don't need a doctor! It's the sick people who do!"

The Child Ego State has various aspects to it. The creative lighthearted behavior can change to fear or anger or grief. The passion feeling rips and claws at our innermost being. Jesus experienced it all.

In the natural state, He desperately cried,

"My soul is crushed with horror and sadness to the point of death . . . stay here . . .

stay awake with me."

Already He was being exposed to rejection. Much more intense was this experience than the laughter from the crowds around the cross. The onlooker would be expected, but the rejection of friends crushes and devours.

My heart is pounding faster as I write these words. I'm hurting because I'm feeling all those times that "friends" turned from me when I needed them. I'm no exception. Stories of people being forsaken in times of distress are as common as life itself.

The dearest friend I have still has a tremble in his voice as he shares a dark time of his life with me. A gentleman, whose life is a trophy to caring and a symbol of integrity, he could recall only one person who stood by him in a time of terrible trial. On a single page of his life a tear had dropped and scarcely no one paused to wipe it away to avoid staining its contents. The ink is blurred because as I listened to him, I realized the pain of his aloneness still haunted him. Fortunately, the page was not torn out. He was secure enough in his own self-worth and friendship with God.

I glanced up at him shyly, almost embarrassed to question as I asked, "No one? Not one person that had attended your Bible studies?" His head shook to say, "No." "But what about all the people you've helped," and before I could continue, his hand touched mine as if to say, "Let's not go any further!"

I renewed my vow secretly to always be available should he need me.

This now seemed cloaked in the regret that I didn't have the privilege of experiencing his healing. That would have been impossible since I didn't know him those moments in the past.

Some did however, and they missed out on a precious opportunity. Similar to that moment in history when the God-Man reached out to his friends and said, "My soul is crushed . . . stay here . . . stay awake with me." They missed an opportunity of a lifetime; an act, an opportunity of an eternity, to emotionally support the Saviour of the world.

Christians are prophets of goodness and truth.

Our message is hope. It is available to us because of love and grace. The death and resurrection of Jesus Christ cuts out the disease. The Balm in Gilead is that ointment that soothes and comforts.

The satisfaction and joy comes in watching the fever dissipate. We can be present when a problem is worked through. Our napkin can wipe away a tear and our head can cause another's to stop shaking. It can be our spirit that strengthens a friend to rise above circumstances.

I'm selfish enough to want to be around for the healing.

I refuse to be in a situation in which I would hear those words,

> *"Sleep on now and take your rest . . . the time has come now. I am betrayed!"*

In Transactional Analysis a supreme value is put on these transactions. That is to say, people communicating with people is an art that must be cultivated if intimacy is to be achieved.

This involves understanding the three ego states, their functions, and their effect on others. A goal that you might wish to set for yourself would be the ability to behave from the position appropriate to any given situation.

To help you accomplish this aim, the following suggestions are given:

1. Make a decision on the worth of effective communication.
2. Come to an understanding of how your relationships can be enhanced through an awareness of ego states and transactions.
3. Begin today to develop your sensitivity. (I would refer you to *Getting To Know You*, by Marjorie Umphrey, Harvest House.)
4. Make a thorough study of Transactional Analysis.
5. Read *Born To Win* by Muriel James as an overall approach to T.A.
6. Join a T.A. group in your area.
7. If you are a member of a church or organization, request a T.A. therapist to conduct a group for other interested people.
8. Try to interest the rest of your family in communication.
9. Let this chapter be a launching pad to your

study of Jesus and His transactions with people.

10. Be sensitive to your own ego states. Are you off balance or do you utilize all three when needed.

10

YOU'RE SCRIPTED—
NOW WHAT?

YOU'RE SCRIPTED-NOW WHAT?

"If you really love me, you'll accept me the way I am." "Judy, I don't want to accept you the way you are. I love you, but I can't stand the messy way you keep the house. You're just not organized. If you really love me, you will change, you will even lose some weight."

The argument continued. But let's take this little slice of conversation and see what we can make of it.

First of all, the conversation is not coping with the real problem. Judy is saying that his love should be unconditional. A love relationship is nurtured and grows because two people have learned to meet each other's needs. The ability to meet those needs depends on several things. The first one is to understand the reasons, motives and needs of the other person's frame of reference.

In T.A. we use a term—scripting. Scripting is defined as a "person's ongoing program for his life drama which dictates where he is going with his life and how he is to get there. It is a drama he compulsively acts out, though his awareness of it may be vague."[14]

Let's return to our opening conversation. The real problem is the definition of the word LOVE. Both people are using the spoken word love from their own specific frame of reference.

Judy was reared in a home where the family script allowed for disorganization, confusion and lack of neatness. She was scripted to believe that love was based on the family outings, doing things together and sharing each other's problems. Tangible or material evidences were not a part of proving her love to someone else.

His family script was oriented toward expressing his love through what he did for the other persons. His mother always kept a neat house and attended to all of the physical needs of the family. The father worked hard and long hours which provided substantial financial support for the family.

Both family scripts were reinforced by the cultures they inhabited throughout their lifetime. Love to Judy was sharing time, experiences and problems. Love to him was *doing*. He experienced love from Judy if she was actively doing something for him—not just giving him her time and attention.

What we are saying here is that many misunderstandings arise because two people use the same word but in the context of two different frames of reference—namely their script.

14. M. James & D. Jongeward, *Born To Win*. (Reading, Mass.: Addison-Wesley) 1971.

Let's pause for just a minute and ask some questions about your frame of reference, particularly in reference to God.

1. Do you expect that God manifests his love toward you because he is always doing something for you?
2. Are you sometimes angry with God because he has not seemingly answered your prayers?
3. Do you feel unaccepted by God because you cannot do for Him what you think you should do?
4. Do you feel depressed or anxious because you feel like a failure in your efforts to please God?

If your answer is "yes" to the above questions, then you are scripted to believe that *love is doing.*

I can hear some of you saying right now, "Well, isn't that what love is about? After all, when I became a Christian old things passed away, all things became new." Of course all things became new and yes, a great part of loving is doing. Still, there is more to loving than these two truths.

When you became a Christian, you did not suddenly have a new script. Our basic scripts are not easily changed. That is a real blessing in many ways. For example, the Bible says,

Bring up a child in the way he should go
and when he is old, he will not depart.

The Scripture has stated if we script our child in a certain way, he will always come back to it somewhere in his life.

Some of you may still repeat, "But what about all

things become new?" our answer to this question is that all of the ingredients that make up a life take on new dimensions.

A new found relationship with God touches every aspect of your personality unveiling the reservoir of potential that may have been untapped and dormant. You may have *new* insights because you have a *new* relationship. You have the potential for viewing life, others and yourself from a renewed perspective.

Did you notice that we said the key to a renewed life is the quality and depth of the relationship? When we have a new relationship, growth takes place. But growth has to be based on something. A plant cannot grow from nothing. There must be a seed. The seed, of course, is the image of God within you.

In reality, we can only love because we have the image of God within us. Scripture supports this by declaring that God is love. Love is not a property of God. *God is love.* However, even though we are born in the image of God and have the seed of love, we must learn to love. Yes, initially others, the "big people" in our early life help us to grow in love. But what if they don't?

Years ago I recall talking with a young man in a penal institution. He related his early life experiences to me. It was a sad, tragic and shocking life. His mother was a prostitute and his father a drunkard. I still recall my thinking and feeling when he left my office. If I tried to tell him about love, how could he understand it? You cannot know love with its warm and tender feelings unless you learn it somewhere. To the best of my ability to evaluate a person, he had grown up in a loveless environment.

Yes, this man had the seed or the word within him, but the ground was infertile, sterile and cold. The seed must be watered and cared for in order to spring into an abundant and purposeful life.

What we are saying here is that the first years of life shape and determine the rest of our life to a large extent. The child initially is a learning, experiencing and other-oriented person. He hears what is said with his feelings, not always with his intellect. Sounds and symbols have a meaning unique and specific to the child. A teddy bear may be his best friend—a T.V. star his greatest hero.

As was mentioned in Chapter 2, a child received injunctions. He may hear, "It's not nice to think." Therefore, to be a thinking person has the quality of badness. This injunction may influence any decision he may make for the rest of his life.

Let me illustrate this point. All of us are faced daily with a multitude of choices. There is choice and counter-choice. What shirt should I wear today? Where should I eat lunch? Which pen should I use to write this manuscript? What should I say?

These all seem like simple decisions to be made and they are. But I have a background in knowing the alternatives that are mine. Think now of the child who has no background in finding alternatives or solutions. He must rely upon that which is said to him. An injunction is an idea or value which is planted in the soil of his mind and emerges as a part of his life-style. Enough of these injunctions combined with all the other influences form a pattern or style of life we call a script.

We must now consider your script. What were the imperatives you experienced as a child and later on as an adult that made you the kind of person you are?

Ask yourself the following questions. Reflect on them. Let the answers come. Don't force them.

1. Why are you such a nice person?
2. What is your single greatest fear?
3. Why do you like a certain kind of food in preference to others?
4. Why do you like a certain color?
5. What is your favorite T.V. program?
6. What is your most pronounced dislike?
7. Why do you like certain odors and are repelled by others?
8. Why do you love a certain person so intensely?

There are practical ways you can change your script. I imagine there are different aspects you would like to change. New Year's resolutions just don't seem to change lives. What can you do?

Try the following suggestions:

1. Be courageous and honest in evaluating yourself.
2. Realize that most scripts are unconscious.
3. Determine what behavior you have that you repeat over and over.

4. Try to determine what are some of the aspects of your life you are most rigid about.
5. Look for areas of your life where you cannot make decisions.
6. Ask yourself why a certain type of person turns you off.
7. Why does a certain kind of person make you feel secure and comfortable?
8. Be brave. Confront your fears. Ask yourself, "Why?"
9. Ask yourself honestly why you are judgmental about certain things and not others.

These are just a few of the suggestions that we can make which will assist you in changing your script. As you uncover more information about yourself, you will find more alternatives for yourself.

Consider yourself, your mind, thinking and feelings as an uncharted planet. Be bold. Take a step for yourself and others by first disclosing yourself to you. In getting to know you, your uncharted planet, you may discover aspects of your life you don't like. You may also discover abilities, talents and resources you never knew existed.

Think about Grandma Moses who never painted until late in life. Masterpieces flowed because she dared to discover that which had laid hidden for years.

Yes, changing scripts requires courage. Some people have chosen to be comfortable and safe in their misery rather than reaching out, even to themselves. We suggested the first prerequisite to changing your script is courage. The first chapter of this book opened with an illustration of a man who made a phone call. That took courage. Simply being willing to experience openness is another form of courage.

Years ago when I first became a Christian I had the initial burning desire to get all the information about God that I could. I read the Bible, asked others about Him, and did a lot of thinking. I recall asking a girl about a particular belief she had. She replied, "I don't know, I've just always heard it stated that way." She was scripted and apparently had little interest in knowing whether she really believed the truth or not.

The Scripture says, "study to show thyself approved." I would paraphrase that to say, "Study to approve of thyself."

Some key words we would like you to include in your practice of living are:
1. Re-decision
2. Disclosure
3. Vulnerability
4. Courage

Any change you make will include these key words. In order to use these words for changing your script, you must ask yourself the following questions:
1. Do I really want to change?
2. Do I dare take the risk?

3. Am I willing to re-experience what I have always taken for granted.
4. Will I attempt to trust someone else?
5. Will I attempt to open up to me?
6. Am I afraid to be afraid?
7. Can I risk what little security I have?

Only you can answer these questions.

A famous philosopher once said, "You cannot step into the same stream twice; the water is always changing." We can make choices to change. Use the Word of God and your own resources. These God directed alternatives are yours. USE THEM. Don't settle for that which doesn't feel good, hurts and is miserable. Dare to change and change to live. Dare to be O.K.

SUGGESTED READING

Berne, Eric. *Games People Play* (New York: Grove Press) 1964.

—————. *Sex In Human Loving* (New York: Simon & Schuster) 1970.

—————. *The Structure and Dynamics of Organizations and Groups* (Philadelphia: J. B. Lippincott Co.) 1963.

—————. *Transactional Analysis In Psychotherapy* (New York: Grove Press, Inc.) 1961.

—————. *What Do You Say After You Say Hello* (New York: Grove) 1972.

Erikson, Erik. *Identity: Youth and Crisis* (New York: W. W. Norton and Co.) 1968.

Goulding, Robert. *New Decisions in Transactional Analysis* (Brunner/Mazel, publishers) 1972.

James, Muriel & Jongeward, D. *Born To Win* (Reading, Mass.: Addison-Wesley) 1973.

James, M. "The Use of Structural Analyses in Pastoral Counseling," Pastoral Psychology, Vol. 19, *187* (Oct. 1968) p. 8.

McCormick, P. *Guide for Use of a Life-Script Questionnaire* (Berkeley: Transactional Pubs, Distributor) 1971.

Muller, Phillipe. *The Tasks of Childhood* (New York: McGraw-Hill Book Co.) 1969.

Perls, F. *The Gestalt Approach and Eye Witness to Therapy* (Ben Lomond: Science and Behavior Books) 1973.

Schiff, Jacqui. *All My Children* (Philadelphia, Pa.: M. Evans and Co., Inc.) 1970.

—————. Cathexis Reader (New York: Harper & Row).

Steiner, Claude. *Games Alcoholics Play:* The Analysis of Life Scripts (New York: Grove Press, Inc.) 1971.

Umphrey, Marjorie. *Getting To Know You* (Irvine: Harvest House) 1977.

—————. Winning the Marriage Game (Tapes), Glendale, Calif.: Life Development Center, 1977.

Woollams, Stanley. *Transactional Analysis In Brief* (Ann Arbor, Michigan: Huron Valley Institute) 1974.